Grade **2**

S0-ACW-822

Scott Foresman

The Grammar & Writing Book

ISBN: 0-328-14636-6

All Rights Reserved. Printed in the United States of America. This publication is protected by Copyright, and permission should be obtained from the publisher prior to any prohibited reproduction, storage in a retrieval system, or transmission in any form by any means, electronic, mechanical, photocopying, recording, or likewise. For information regarding permission(s), write to: Permissions Department, Scott Foresman, 1900 East Lake Avenue, Glenview, Illinois 60025.

9 10 V008 09

PEARSON

Scott
Foresman

Editorial Offices: Glenview, Illinois • Parsippany, New Jersey • New York, New York
Sales Offices: Boston, Massachusetts • Duluth, Georgia • Glenview, Illinois
Coppell, Texas • Sacramento, California • Mesa, Arizona

Table of Contents

Writer's Guide

Rubrics and Models

Check Your Writing

Grammar and Writing Lessons

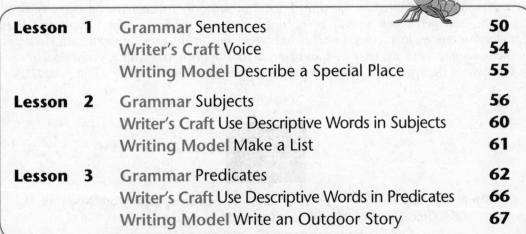

Writing for Tests

Grammar Patrol

Index

Writer's Guide

Focus/Ideas

Good writers **focus** on a **main idea.** They give details about this idea. They also keep in mind their **purpose.** The purpose may be to persuade someone, teach something, or make the reader laugh.

A thank-you note has a main idea and a purpose.

Dear Aunt Ani,

    Thank you so much for my great birthday present. The set of markers is terrific! I'll draw a picture just for you.

Jamie

Main Idea   To say that you liked a present

Purpose   To thank your aunt for the present

Details   Details add information. Be sure all details focus on your main idea.

Strategies for Focus and Ideas

- Choose a topic you can support with details.

- Keep focused on your topic.

A **Match** the number of each topic with the purpose that it fits best.

A   Make someone laugh

B   Persuade

C   Give information

1. Why people should help with the park clean-up

2. A silly trick my brother played

3. What birds do in winter

B **Read** the main-idea sentence. Then **write** the numbers of any details that do not focus on the main idea.

Main Idea   The zoo has many interesting animals.

4. The zebra looks like a black and white horse.

5. The monkeys chatter happily.

6. Cows are useful farm animals.

7. The elephant has a long trunk.

8. My town has many interesting sights.

Improving Focus/Ideas

Original

Tigers are in the cat family. They are much larger than pet cats. A tiger might weigh 400 pounds. It can be 9 feet long. Tigers are my favorite animals. They have interesting striped coats. Wild tigers live in India and other places in Asia. Tigers hunt at night. They can leap very far to catch their prey. Tigers could die out. That would be a shame! Find out how tigers are different from lions. Tigers are so beautiful.

Revising Tips

Add a main-idea sentence that gets readers' attention. (*Have you ever seen a 400-pound cat?*)

Use only details that focus on the main idea. (*Tigers are my favorite animals* tells about the writer. It doesn't tell about tigers.)

Use lively, interesting words. (*They have brown or orange coats with black stripes* paints a clear picture.)

Keep your purpose in mind. Take out the sentence that begins *Find out...* because it doesn't inform.

Improved

Have you ever seen a 400-pound cat? If you have seen a tiger, you have. Tigers are in the cat family. But they are much larger than pet cats. They can be 9 feet long. Tigers are beautiful because they have interesting colors. They have brown or orange coats with black stripes. Wild tigers live in India and in other places in Asia. Tigers hunt at night. They can leap very far to catch their prey. Tigers could die out because people hunt them. That would be a shame! Tigers are strong and beautiful animals.

Writer's Corner

Your main idea sentence is like a camera lens. Use it to focus your paper. If any detail does not make the main idea clearer, take it out.

Organization/Paragraphs

> A good writer tells what happens in the right order. Your **organization** holds your writing together.

Here are some ways to organize your writing.

- A story with a beginning, middle, and end
- A paragraph that compares and contrasts
- A description
- A how-to explanation

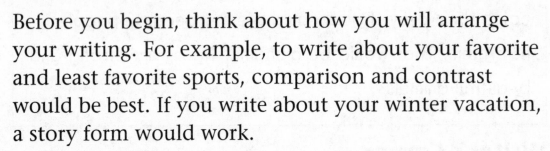

Before you begin, think about how you will arrange your writing. For example, to write about your favorite and least favorite sports, comparison and contrast would be best. If you write about your winter vacation, a story form would work.

Once you decide, choose the details you want to use. Arrange your details from beginning to end.

Strategies for Organizing Ideas

- Begin a paragraph with a topic sentence that tells the main idea.
- Start or finish with the most important detail.
- Use order words such as *first*, *later*, *last*, and *next*.

A **Match** the number of the topic with the letter of the kind of organization that works best.

A   Comparison-Contrast

B   Description

C   Story

D   How-to Explanation

1. How to Make a Clay Pot

2. A Funny Event at the School Fair

3. My Garden in Spring

4. Hockey or Soccer: Which Is Better?

B **Write** the sentences about learning to ride a bike. **Put** them in correct order to tell what happened.

5. Second, David gave me a push.

6. Finally, David let go and I rode by myself.

7. Next, David held the seat while I pedaled.

8. First, David held the bike while I got on.

C **Tell** how to do an outdoor activity. **Use** order words such as *first*, *then*, and *next* to organize the details.

Improving Organization

Original

My teacher held me so I floated. I put all the actions together. I moved my arms in long strokes. I kicked my legs up and down. I practiced moving my head to one side. I learned to take a breath each time I moved my head. I swam all the way across the pool.

Revising Tips

Include a topic sentence that tells your main idea.   (Start with *Last summer I learned how to swim.*)

Organize details in the correct order.   When you tell how you did something, put events in time order. (*I put all the actions together* should come later.)

Use order words such as *first, then,* and *next* to make the steps clear.   (*First, my teacher held me so I floated.*)

Tie ideas together in your conclusion.   (*Before long, I had reached an important goal* tells why the event was important to the writer.)

Improved

Last summer I learned how to swim. First, my teacher held me so I floated. Soon I could float all by myself. Next, I moved my arms in long strokes. I kicked my legs up and down with all my strength. Then the teacher showed me how to move my head to one side. I learned to take a breath each time I moved my head. Finally, I put all the actions together. Before long, I had reached an important goal. I could swim all the way across the pool!

Writer's Corner

Include vivid details. For example, don't just say *kicked up and down*. If you say *kicked up and down with all my strength,* your story comes alive.

Voice

Your writing style shows your **voice**. It tells how you feel and think about your topic. Your writer's voice shows that you know and care about your topic. It lets you speak directly to the reader.

- When I saw my new kitten, I was happy. (weak voice)
- I squealed with delight when I saw that furry little face. (strong voice)

Strategies for Developing a Writer's Voice

- Think about your readers and your reason for writing. Use a playful voice to write about a funny event. Use a more serious voice in a book report.

- Choose words that match your voice. In a letter to a friend, contractions or funny words would sound like your everyday voice. A letter to your principal would have a more serious voice.

- Your writing voice is a way that you can speak directly to your readers. Let readers know how you feel about a subject.

A **Match** each opening sentence with the letter of the reader it fits best.

A My cousin Louis

B The mayor of my town

C Students in my school

1. Support me for class president! You won't be sorry.

2. Thank you for letting us help plan the parade.

3. I played the coolest game last weekend.

B **Write** *S* for the sentence that shows a strong voice. **Write** *W* for the sentence that shows a weak voice.

4. I never knew ice skating could be so much fun!

5. I can ice skate.

C **Complete** one of these opening sentences. **Add** sentences to write a paragraph about that topic. **Use** a voice that fits your topic.

- When I do chores, I ___.

- The best thing I ever ate was ___.

- Here are some simple steps for ___.

Improving Voice

Original

Dear Ms. Jenkins,

   We want to have a special Presidents' Day program. It would be awesome! We could sing that song about the presidents. You said we sang it great. I'll work on it before the program. Each person could tell about one president. Our parents could come and everything. We could serve refreshments. Remember the fruit salad James brought last time? Please, could we?

Tara Roberts

Revising Tips

Think about your reader and your reason for writing. When you write a persuasive letter to a teacher or principal, use a serious voice. (*It would be awesome* would be better in a letter to a friend.)

Use words that match your purpose. (Replace contractions such as *I'll* and unclear expressions such as *could come and everything*.)

Make your voice strong and clear. (*Please, could we?* sounds like begging instead of being persuasive.)

Improved

Dear Ms. Jenkins,

Our class would like to have a special Presidents' Day program. We could sing the song about the presidents that we learned. Each person could tell something about a president. Some people might even dress up like George Washington or Abraham Lincoln. We could invite our parents and serve refreshments. This would be a great way to learn. We could have fun at the same time. I hope we can plan this special program.

Tara Roberts

Writer's Corner

Read your paper out loud to yourself. Does it sound like you? Change the places where the voice does not sound natural.

Word Choice

Choose your **words** carefully to add style to your writing. Use exact nouns, strong verbs, and exciting adjectives. They will make your work interesting, clear, and lively.

- The pet of my friend is nice. (wordy and dull)
- My friend's Siamese cat plopped onto my lap. (lively and exact)

Strategies for Choosing the Right Words

- Choose exact nouns. (*sandal* instead of *shoe*)

- Use strong verbs. (*clattered* instead of *made a noise*)

- Replace dull words such as *nice, bad,* and *thing* with clear words. (*My head felt achy and hot* instead of *My head felt bad*)

- Include words that give readers pictures. (*The lemonade made my mouth pucker* instead of *The lemonade was sour*)

- Don't be wordy. (*because* instead of *the reason was because*)

A **Choose** the more exact word in ( ) to complete each sentence. **Write** each sentence.

(1) The boys and girls (walk, stroll) in the park. (2) The trees are full of (robins, birds). (3) They (chirp, call) in the bright sunshine. (4) (Flowers, Daisies) grow in the field. (5) They look (nice, cheerful).

B **Choose** a word from the box to replace each underlined word. **Write** the sentences.

golden	shouted	cast
pond	leaped	

6. Tom and Dan put their boat on the <u>water</u>.

7. A fish suddenly <u>came</u> out.

8. The fish looked <u>bright</u>.

9. Tom <u>spoke</u>.

10. Dan <u>put</u> his fishing line in to catch the fish.

C **Write** a description of a flower or tree that you like. **Use** strong, exact words to make your writing come alive.

Improving Word Choice

Original

Our town had a big bicycle race. The riders were all
ages. They went through town. Then they raced on two
country roads that went through the countryside. My
family and I watched the people go down Main Street.
They wore bright shirts. They went fast. I liked the way
the racers looked in a big group. Everybody in town
liked the race.

Revising Tips

Choose exact nouns.   (*racers* instead of *people*)

Use strong verbs.   (*zip* instead of *go*)

Replace dull words with clear ones.   (*They looked
like a big swarm of colorful bees* instead of *I liked the way
the racers looked in a big group.*)

Include words that use our senses.   (*Each racer
wore a bright shirt of red, yellow, or blue.*)

Don't be wordy.   Rewrite sentences that contain
words you don't need. (Make the fourth sentence
clearer and more specific.)

Improved

Our town had an exciting bicycle race. Young and old bicycle riders raced through town. Then they raced uphill, downhill, and curved around two country roads. My family and I watched the racers zip down Main Street. Each racer wore a bright shirt of red, yellow, or blue. The racers whooshed by. They looked like a big swarm of colorful bees. The crowds on the sidewalk clapped and cheered for the racers.

Writer's Corner

Take time to pick the best words. As you write, close your eyes and picture in your mind what you are describing. What words can bring the object or event to life?

Sentences

Good writers use different kinds of **sentences**. This gives the writing rhythm and style. A mix of short and longer sentences lets your writing flow.

Here are some ways to improve your sentences.

- Use questions, exclamations, and commands.

- Don't use only short, choppy sentences. Longer sentences can help your writing sound smooth.

- Use different beginnings. Too many sentences that begin with *I*, *she*, *the*, or *a* can be boring.

- Combine short sentences with connecting words such as *and*, *or*, or *but* to make them flow better.

Strategies for Improving Your Sentences

Use a checklist as you edit your writing:

- Circle sentences that begin with *I, the, he,* or *a.*

- Underline short, choppy sentences.

- List the different kinds of sentences you used.

- Now look at your sentences. Make changes to improve your sentences.

A **Use** the connecting word in ( ) to join the two sentences. **Add** a comma and change a capital letter. **Write** the sentences.

Example   I can skate. I cannot swim. (but)
                 I can skate, but I cannot swim.

1. I take the bus to school. I ride my bike. (or)

2. Dad drove to the lake. We rode on a boat. (and)

3. I like trains. I have never ridden on one. (but)

B **Rearrange** the words in each sentence so that it begins with the underlined words. **Write** the sentences.

Example   We drove to Milwaukee <u>last summer</u>.
                 Last summer we drove to Milwaukee.

(4) The family goes to the beach <u>each year</u>.
(5) The seashore gets very crowded <u>in June</u>.
(6) The dog will come too <u>this summer</u>.

C **Describe** a place you visited and how you got there. **Use** different kinds of sentences. **Begin** each sentence with a different word.

Improving Sentences

Original

I went bowling last Saturday. It was my first time. I used the lightest ball. It still felt heavy. I rolled the ball down the alley. It went into the gutter. I rolled it again. It went into the gutter too. I finally started to get the hang of the game. I rolled the ball again. I knocked down five pins. I rolled the ball right down the center of the alley next time. I knocked down all ten pins. I scored a strike.

Revising Tips

Combine choppy sentences with connecting words. (*I used the lightest ball, but it still felt heavy.*)

Use different beginnings. Don't always start with the subject of the sentence. (*Last Saturday I went bowling* instead of *I went bowling last Saturday*)

Use questions, exclamations, and commands as well as statements. (*I scored my first strike!*)

Use both short and longer sentences.

Improved

Last Saturday I went bowling for the first time. I used the lightest ball, but it still felt heavy. I rolled the ball down the alley, and it went into the gutter. The next time I rolled the ball, it went into the gutter again. Finally, I started to get the hang of the game. I rolled the ball again. Would you believe I knocked down five pins? Next time, I rolled the ball right down the center of the alley. All ten pins toppled over. I scored my first strike!

Writer's Corner

Here is a good way to get your readers interested. Start your paper with a question. People will keep reading to find out the answer!

Conventions

Conventions are the rules for writing.

- jack plast the babe roben bak in the nest (weak)
- Jack placed the baby robin back in the nest. (strong)

Strategies for Conventions in Writing

- Start each sentence with a capital letter. End sentences with an end punctuation mark.

- Each sentence should tell a complete idea. Use the correct verbs to go with singular and plural nouns.

- Use correct verb tenses.

- Follow the rules for punctuation marks.

- Spell all words correctly.

- Use pronouns correctly.

Proofreading Marks

¶ New paragraph
≡ Capital letter
/ Lowercase letter
○ Correct the spelling.
∧ Add something.
℅ Remove something.

A **Choose** the correct word in ( ) to complete each sentence. **Write** the sentences.

1. (Me, I) kicked the soccer ball all morning.

2. Mike (saw, seen) me score a goal.

3. Mike (say, says) that I am a good player.

4. I will play on a team next (year, yeer).

B Each sentence has one mistake. **Correct** the mistake and **write** the paragraph.

(5) It was time for the soccer game? **(6)** the teams stood on the field in their bright shirts. **(7)** One player kicks the ball. **(8)** My friend peter blocked the kick.

C **Write** three sentences about one of the topics below. **Follow** the rules for capitalization, punctuation, grammar, and spelling. **Trade** papers with a partner. Proofread each other's work.

- My favorite outdoor game
- A person who is good at a sport
- An activity for a rainy day

Improving Conventions

Original

> Do you have any pets. Then you might know my Neighbor, dr. Mason. She is an animal docter. She cares for pets. She takes care of dogs and cats. Sometimes takes care of hamsters. When we got a new cat, we took her to dr Mason. She cheks to make sure fluffy was healthy. Then she gives her some shots. I woud like to be a animal docter like dr Mason when I grow up.

Revising Tips

Check for correct capitalization. Do not capitalize common nouns.   (*neighbor* instead of *Neighbor, Dr.* instead of *dr., Fluffy* instead of *fluffy*)

Make sure each sentence has a subject and a verb.   (*Sometimes <u>she</u> takes care of hamsters.*)

Use verb tenses correctly.   (*She <u>checked</u> to make sure Fluffy was healthy. Then she <u>gave</u> her some shots.*)

Use correct end punctuation.   (*Do you have any pets?* instead of *Do you have any pets.*)

Check spelling.   (*docter, cheks, woud*)

Improved

Do you have any pets? Then you might know my neighbor, Dr. Mason. She is an animal doctor. She cares for people's pets. She takes care of dogs and cats. Sometimes she takes care of hamsters. When we got a new cat, we took her to Dr. Mason. She checked to make sure Fluffy was healthy. Then she gave her some shots. I would like to be an animal doctor like Dr. Mason when I grow up.

Writer's Corner

When you proofread, look for one mistake at a time. For example, look for correct capital letters first. Then look for correct punctuation. Then look for spelling errors.

Rubrics and Models

Narrative Writing *Scoring Rubric*

A scoring **rubric** can be used to judge a piece of writing. A rubric is a checklist of traits, or writing skills, to look for. See pages 2–25 for a discussion of these traits. Rubrics give a number score for each trait.

Score	4	3	2	1
Focus/Ideas	Detailed ideas on topic; beginning, middle, and end	Good story; details mostly about topic	Unfocused story with some details not on topic	Unclear story with many details not on topic
Organization/ Paragraphs	Ideas easy to follow, with order words	Details given in some order	Details not in clear order	No order
Voice	Lively and shows writer's feelings	Mostly lively and shows writer's feelings	Not lively; little or no feelings	Careless with no feelings
Word Choice	Vivid, clear word pictures	Good word picture	No word pictures	Incorrect, dull, or overused words
Sentences	Smooth sentences; different kinds	Most sentences smooth; some different kinds	Many stringy or choppy sentences	Hard to understand, not complete, or choppy
Conventions	Few or no errors	No serious errors	Many errors	Too many errors

Following are four models that respond to a prompt. Each model has been given a score, based on the rubric.

Writing Prompt Write a story about a surprise that a character has. The character may be a person or an animal.

Narrative Writing Model *Score 4*

Robbie was a rabbit. Robbie's mother gave Robbie two carrots each day. He ate lettuce and peppers too. Robbie liked carrots best. One day Robbie headed home. He had hopped in the fields all day. He was hungry for a snack. Robbie walked into his little rabbit home. Then seven rabbits jumped out. They said, "Surprise!" It was Robbie's birthday! Can you guess what Robbie's friends gave him for a present? Carrots! It was the best surprise ever!

Focus/Ideas Focused on the event; many details

Organization/Paragraphs Order words show time order (*One day, Then*)

Voice Shows writer's imagination and personality

Word Choice Exact word choice and word pictures (*hopped, little rabbit home*)

Sentences Different sentence kinds and lengths

Conventions Excellent spelling, grammar, and punctuation

Narrative Writing Model *Score 3*

One day Rosa walked home from school. She liked looking at flowers. She forgot her lunchbox. Rosa hurried back to school. No lunchbox! Poor Rosa was sad. She went home and told her mom. Rosa's mom said she wood get Rosa a new lunchbox. The next day her mom gived her a big paper bag. Rosa looks inside. It's a new lunchbox. Just like her old lunchbox! Rosa wood never forget her lunchbox again.

Focus/Ideas   Focused on character's experience; one sentence off topic (*She liked looking at flowers.*)

Organization/Paragraphs   Details in time order

Voice   Writer's feelings revealed (*Poor Rosa was sad.*)

Word Choice   Uses some vivid words (*forgot, hurried, big paper bag*)

Sentences   Many sentences begin with *Rosa* or *she*.

Conventions   Errors in verb forms and tense (*her mom gived; Rosa looks; It's*); spelling error (*wood*); fragments

Narrative Writing Model *Score 2*

Tommy's surprise was he got to go to the city. He never went there before. All his freinds had went. Tommy saw big bildings buses and peple. He ate lunch there he saw anemels at the zoo. A lion a tiger a monkey were some of the anemels. Tommy had a good surprise.

Focus/Ideas   Focused on the experience; one sentence off topic (*All his freinds had went.*)

Organization/Paragraphs   No clear beginning, middle, and end

Voice   Few feelings expressed

Word Choice   Includes specific nouns (*lion, tiger, monkey*); needs vivid adjectives

Sentences   Needs some different lengths; could use a question or an exclamation

Conventions   Many misspellings (*freinds, bildings, peple, anemels*); errors in verb forms (*freinds had went*); run-on sentence; commas missing in series

Narrative Writing Model *Score 1*

James was a boy he got a new bike. His mom and dad give it to him for his brithday. Its blue my bikes red. He go fast on the bike. I like suprises.

Focus/Ideas   Topic not presented clearly; few details

Organization/Paragraphs   Unclear order; no beginning, middle, and end

Voice   Little sense of writer's personality

Word Choice   Limited, dull word choice

Sentences   No variety of length or type

Conventions   Subject-verb agreement errors (*He go*); verb tense shifts (*got a new bike; His mom and dad give; Its blue*); misspellings (*brithday, Its, bikes, suprises*); run-on sentences

Descriptive Writing *Scoring Rubric*

Score	4	3	2	1
Focus/Ideas	Focused ideas on topic; excellent description	Good description; details mostly focused on topic	Description not focused, with some details not on topic	Ideas not clear or on descriptive topic; few details
Organization/ Paragraphs	Ideas easy to follow and in some order	Details given in some order	Little order	No order
Voice	Lively writing; shows writer's feelings	Mostly lively; shows writer's feelings	Not lively; little or no feeling	Careless with no feeling
Word Choice	Vivid, clear word pictures that appeal to senses	Good word pictures; some appeal to senses	Dull word pictures	Incorrect, dull, or overused words
Sentences	Smooth sentences; some different kinds	Most sentences smooth; some different kinds	Many stringy or choppy sentences	Hard to understand, not complete, or choppy
Conventions	Few or no errors	No serious errors	Many errors	Too many errors

Following are four models that respond to a prompt. Each model has been given a score, based on the rubric.

Writing Prompt Describe your favorite kind of weather. Use precise nouns and vivid adjectives to help your reader see, hear, and feel the weather.

Descriptive Writing Model *Score 4*

Snowy days are my favorite weather. The sky is a pale gray, and the whole world looks white. The air feels as cold as a freezer. Snowflakes float slowly through the air. Soon they cover the ground. It is quiet because the snow doesn't make any noise. The only sounds are when I walk across the snowy ground. My boots squeak in the snow. I love snowy days.

Focus/Ideas   Strong focus on the weather with many supporting details

Organization/Paragraphs   Clear introduction and conclusion; logical order of details

Voice   Shows love of season

Word Choice   Vivid words and phrases that appeal to senses (*pale gray, as cold as a freezer, squeak*)

Sentences   Clear sentences of different lengths; however, several beginning with *the*

Conventions   Excellent grammar, spelling, and punctuation

Descriptive Writing Model *Score 3*

Windy weather makes things move. You can feel the wind blow across your face. It blows your hair all around. You can see the wind blow the tree brachs. It can blow trash and other things around too. People should pick up the litter. You can fly a kite in the wind or you can take a walk. You feel like the wind might blow you over. Its fun to go outside on a windy day.

Focus/Ideas   Many details about topic; one sentence off topic (*People should pick up the litter.*)

Organization/Paragraphs Good introduction and ending

Voice   Sense of writer's personality

Word Choice   Some word pictures (*fly a kite in the wind*); some words not exact (*other things*); some repetition (*blow, blows, you can*)

Sentences   Needs different lengths and kinds; too many sentences beginning with *You*

Conventions   A few mistakes; some spelling errors (*brachs, Its*)

Descriptive Writing Model *Score 2*

Sunny wether is the best wether you can go to the beach. The sun feel nice and hot. And the sky is kind of brit. Sometimes you get real hot, but its still nice. You could cool of in the warter. The warter in the oshun tastes like salt. Be careful in the waves.

Focus/Ideas   Some details on topic; last two sentences off the topic

Organization/Paragraphs   Good beginning; needs conclusion that sums up topic

Voice   Shows some feelings about sunny weather

Word Choice   Some word pictures (*tastes like salt*); some dull words (*nice*); sometimes general (*kind of*)

Sentences   Some differences in length

Conventions   Many misspellings (*wether, brit, its, of, warter, oshun*); error in subject-verb agreement (*The sun feel*); run-on sentence

Descriptive Writing Model *Score 1*

Rain is good some times. Everything get wet and you have stay inside and play vidio games and some you could play a bord game with Mom and Dad. What is your faverit. Theres pudels in the yard thats why you have to play in side. I dont like rain all the time but rain is good and it maks trees grow and thats why rain is good.

Focus/Ideas   Paragraph not a clear description of the weather; sentence off the topic (*What is your faverit.*)

Organization/Paragraphs   No clear sense of order

Voice   Doesn't show writer's personality

Word Choice   Dull word choice (*good, is*); no word pictures; repetition (*Rain is good.*)

Sentences   Too many *ands*

Conventions   Many misspellings; some words left out (*you have stay inside; some you could*); incorrect end punctuation; error in subject-verb agreement (*Everything get*); run-on sentence

Persuasive Writing *Scoring Rubric*

Score	4	3	2	1
Focus/Ideas	Clear opinion; good reasons used to persuade	Clear opinion; reasons help persuade	Opinion not always clear or on persuasive topic; few reasons	Ideas not clear or on persuasive topic; no reasons
Organization/ Paragraphs	Good introduction and conclusion	Facts given in some order	Order not clear	No order
Voice	Lively writing; shows writer's feelings	Mostly lively; shows writer's feelings	Not lively; little or no feeling	Careless with no feeling
Word Choice	Good use of persuasive words	Some use of persuasive words	Few persuasive words	Dull word choice; no persuasive words
Sentences	Smooth sentences of different lengths and kinds	Most sentences smooth; some different lengths and kinds	Many stringy or choppy sentences	Hard to understand, not complete, or choppy
Conventions	Few or no errors	No serious errors	Many errors	Too many errors

Following are four models that respond to a prompt. Each model has been given a score, based on the rubric.

Writing Prompt   Think about a special activity for the students in your class. Write a letter to your teacher. Persuade him or her to have the activity.

Persuasive Writing Model *Score 4*

Dear Ms. Murray,

    Our class should have an arts and crafts fair. Some people could draw pictures. Some people could make clay bowls, and some could make kites or birds out of paper. Then we can display all the art and crafts around our classroom. We can invite the other students to come look. Maybe we could have prizes. Everyone would have fun. I think everyone would love an arts and crafts fair.

Yours truly,

Mark Shaw

Focus/Ideas   Clear opinion; many persuasive details

Organization/Paragraphs   Strong introduction and conclusion help persuade

Voice   Shows writer's feelings about topic

Word Choice   Uses persuasive words (*should, fun*)

Sentences   Clear sentences of different lengths

Conventions   Excellent grammar, spelling, and punctuation

Persuasive Writing Model *Score 3*

Dear Mr. Ochoa,

    May we have a school game day? The students at Roosevelt school could run in short and long races. We could also have relay races for teams. Each team with three or four people. We could have jumping and thowing to see who could jump the highest and thow the longest. A game day would really help school spirit! It would help everyone get in shape too.

                              Yours truly,

                              Alicia Adams

Focus/Ideas   Clear request; many persuasive details

Organization/Paragraphs   Order of importance of reasons not always clear

Voice   Shows some excitement; needs personality

Word Choice   Some persuasive words (*help*)

Sentences   Includes question and exclamation

Conventions   Capitalization error; spelling errors (*thowing, thow*); fragment

Persuasive Writing Model *Score 2*

Dear Mrs. Kaufman

    We should have a inter national day. That's when evryone brings food from another contry. Or something else. You could choose france or Mexico then you put it all around. Evryone gets to look at the stuff and learn.

Your friend,

Toby Rice

Focus/Ideas Focused on the request; needs more focused reasons

Organization/Paragraphs Details need clear order; no clear ending

Voice No clear writer's voice

Word Choice Unclear (*or something else, put it all around, stuff*); some persuasive words

Sentences Choppy and stringy sentences

Conventions Several misspellings; capitalization error (*france*); incorrect word (*a inter national*); no comma after greeting; fragment; run-on sentence

Persuasive Writing Model *Score 1*

Dear Mr. Line

Cold we go to the water park before schools out because its real fun. Well, my grandma lives near the water park and one time she took us their then we spent the night their then we got up. Slideing on the slides. And, other things. we shold go to the water park because its fun.

Jenny Fong

Focus/Ideas Includes many details not about topic

Organization/Paragraphs No clear order

Voice No clear writer's voice

Word Choice Unclear words (*And, other things*); repeated words (*fun*)

Sentences Stringy sentence

Conventions Misspellings; apostrophe errors; capitalization error; run-on; no comma after greeting; no closing; fragments

Expository Writing *Scoring Rubric*

Score	4	3	2	1
Focus/Ideas	Clear topic with many facts; excellent explanation	Good explanation; clear ideas with some facts	Explanation not always clear or on topic; few facts	Explanation not clear or on topic; few or no facts
Organization/ Paragraphs	Ideas easy to follow	Facts given in some order	Unclear order	No order
Voice	Shows writer's feelings, but serious	Mostly serious; shows writer's feelings	Not lively; little or no feeling	Careless with no feeling
Word Choice	Clear, well-chosen words	Words mostly well chosen	Words sometimes not fitting topic	Words often not fitting topic
Sentences	Smooth sentences of different lengths and kinds	Most sentences smooth; some different lengths and kinds	Many stringy or choppy sentences	Hard to understand, not complete, or choppy
Conventions	Few or no errors	No serious errors	Many errors	Too many errors

Following are four models that respond to a prompt. Each model has been given a score, based on the rubric.

Writing Prompt   Write about a holiday that Americans celebrate. Support your main idea with facts about the holiday.

Expository Writing Model *Score 4*

The Fourth of July is an important holiday for us. It started in 1776. That's when America became free from England. On the Fourth of July, there are many parades. People from the Army and Navy march in the parade. Bands play American music. Flags are everywhere. People have picnics and cook outside with their friends and families. At night, they watch beautiful fireworks. They remind Americans of their freedom.

Focus/Ideas   Main idea clearly presented; supported with many facts and details

Organization/Paragraphs   Clear order of details; good beginning and ending

Voice   Friendly but serious voice

Word Choice   Specific word choice (*People from the Army and Navy, beautiful fireworks*)

Sentences   Clear sentences of different lengths and varied beginnings

Conventions   Excellent grammar, spelling, and punctuation

Expository Writing Model *Score 3*

> Americans celebrate Thanksgiving to show we love our country. The holiday reminds people of the Pilgrims. They came from england in the 1600s. Their boat was the <u>Mayflower</u>. They settled in Masatchusets. They had a hard time, but the Indians helped them. They learned to grow food. They had a big feast because they were happy. Today Americans have Thanksgiving each november. We eat turkey, potatoes, and pumpkin pie. We are thankful for our country. We remember the Pilgrims and Indians.

Focus/Ideas   Clear main idea in first sentence; many supporting details, some off topic (*the <u>Mayflower</u>*)

Organization/Paragraphs   Needs order words

Voice   Serious voice; could show more feelings

Word Choice   Exact, clear nouns (*feast, turkey*)

Sentences   Many choppy and begin with *They* or *We*

Conventions   Some capitalization and spelling errors (*england, Masatchusets, november*)

Expository Writing Model *Score 2*

Do you like to selbrate Presidents day. Presidents day is a American holiday. I like it because it is selbrateing some presidents Washington Lincoln and others and they all helped our country. We put flags on our house sometimes so we rember our great presidents. We get a day off school.

Focus/Ideas   Main idea clear; focus unclear at end; needs more details about holiday

Organization/Paragraphs   Good introduction; details need better order; stronger conclusion needed

Voice   Writer shows personality

Word Choice   Unclear words (*and others*)

Sentences   One stringy sentence; some different sentence kinds and lengths

Conventions   Misspellings (*selbrate, rember*); missing commas in series; error in end punctuation; capitalization and apostrophe errors (*Presidents day*); incorrect word (*a American*)

Expository Writing Model *Score 1*

My best holiday is fun. Gess what it is. Its in febuary you allways have a school party and then you take you valentines home and then you show them to your mom. And you can make your own decratons at home too. Everyone give valentines to there friends and eat treats and have valentines parties. Decrate with harts and have a party. It is fun.

Focus/Ideas   Main idea not presented clearly

Organization/Paragraphs   No clear order; needs strong conclusion

Voice   Strong voice

Word Choice   Repeated words (*fun*); dull; few specific words

Sentences   Long, stringy sentences; hard to understand

Conventions   Many misspellings; subject-verb agreement error; error in end punctuation; errors with apostrophes and capitalization; wrong pronoun; fragment and run-on sentence

Check Your Writing

Check your writing by reading it over carefully. Try the following strategies.

Read your work aloud.

- If it sounds choppy, combine short sentences.
- Rewrite a long, stringy sentence as several sentences.
- Sentences should not all begin with *the* or *I*.
- Do ideas seem connected? If not, add words such as *then*, *next*, or *but*.

Check your style. It should match your audience and purpose.   You might begin an e-mail to a friend, "Hey, you won't believe the cool thing that happened." For a test, the following would be a better beginning: "An unusual thing happened today."

Be sure you have answered the prompt.

- Look for key words in the writing prompt.

  Compare a bike and a car. Tell two ways they are alike and two ways they are different.

  Topic: bike and car
  What you need to do: Compare
  What to include: Two likenesses and two differences

Make sure your writing is focused. Take out sentences that are off the subject.

Check that there is enough support.

- Use details to give readers pictures.
- Support your opinion with reasons.
- Explain a main idea with good details.

Do you have a strong beginning? Does a question, a surprising fact, or an interesting detail get a reader's interest?

Is your ending good? A conclusion may say the main idea in a new way, tell what you have learned, or ask a question.

Check that you have used good words—and not too many of them.

- Strong verbs, precise nouns, and vivid adjectives make your writing clear and lively.
- Replace wordy phrases such as *blue in color* with *blue* and *in a careful way* with *carefully*.

Checklist

- [ ] My writing sounds smooth and easy to read.

- [ ] I have used a good style for my audience and purpose.

- [ ] My writing answers the prompt or assignment.

- [ ] My writing is focused.

- [ ] I have used enough support.

- [ ] I have a strong beginning.

- [ ] I have a satisfying conclusion.

- [ ] I have used good words and avoided wordiness.

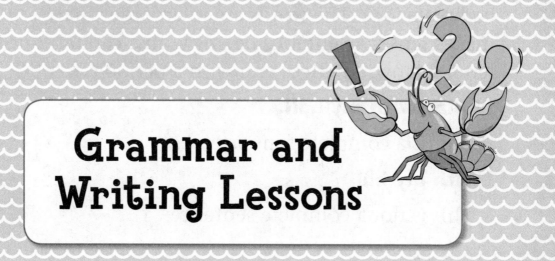

Grammar and Writing Lessons

Sentences

A **sentence** is a group of words that tells a complete idea. The words are in an order that makes sense. A sentence begins with a capital letter. Many sentences end with a period **(.)**.

I play with my ball.

This is a complete sentence.

with my ball

This is not a complete sentence.

A **Find** the sentence. **Write** the sentence.

1. the ball   I throw the ball.

2. Walter catches it.   catches it

3. My friend has a pony.   a pony

4. rides the pony   He rides the pony.

5. Walter is my friend.   my friend

B **Put** each group of words in order to make a sentence. **Write** the sentences.

1. are blooming. The roses

2. birds Some are singing.

3. is tall. The tree

4. at night. Stars shine

5. fast. The pony runs

6. was fun. The farm

C **Add** a word or words from the box to make each group of words a sentence. **Write** the sentences.

is in a tree	Squirrels	brings games with her
The house	climb up a ladder	Dad

7. The little house ___.

8. ___ is made of wood.

9. Iris and I ___.

10. ___ run by.

11. Iris ___.

12. ___ makes us lunch.

Test Preparation

✓ **Write** the letter of the sentence.

1. ○ **A** Grandpa milks the cows.
   ○ **B** Milk from the cows.
   ○ **C** Grandpa with the cows.

2. ○ **A** Walter for a visit.
   ○ **B** Walter comes for a visit.
   ○ **C** Walter and the visit.

3. ○ **A** Rides the pony.
   ○ **B** Barb rides the pony.
   ○ **C** The fast pony.

4. ○ **A** Grandma the corn.
   ○ **B** Corn on the cob.
   ○ **C** Grandma picks corn.

5. ○ **A** Pete counts the stars.
   ○ **B** Counts the stars.
   ○ **C** The stars for Pete.

6. ○ **A** Ann with skates.
   ○ **B** The new skates.
   ○ **C** Ann has new skates.

Review

✓ **Write** the group of words that is a sentence.

1. The birds in the house.
   We look at the birds.

2. Zack runs fast.
   Zack on a ladder.

3. The spider in the web.
   The spider spins a web.

4. Matt in the park.
   Matt explores the park.

✓ **Choose** the word that makes the group of words a sentence. **Write** each sentence.

5. Alex ___ on the door.
   Sue   knocks   friends

6. A ___ lives in the woods.
   climb   stop   bear

7. Mom ___ at the joke.
   smiles   horse   Dru

8. The ___ pet the pony.
   stays   children   jump

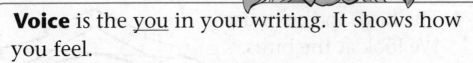

Voice

> **Voice** is the <u>you</u> in your writing. It shows how you feel.
>
> | | |
> |---|---|
> | **Weak Voice** | I ate all my dinner. |
> | **Strong Voice** | I gobbled up every tasty bite. |

Which sentence in each pair tells how the writer feels? **Write** the sentence.

1. I got a red dress yesterday.
   This red dress is my favorite.

2. Exercise makes me feel good.
   I exercise every morning before school.

3. Our family has a kitten.
   I love this playful kitten.

4. Tears poured down my face after the movie.
   The movie was sad.

5. I shook with fear inside the dark cave.
   I went inside the dark cave.

 Write about a time when you were scared. **Use** words that show readers how you felt and acted.

Describe a Special Place

Writing Prompt Write about your special place. Tell what you see and do there.

Aunt Maya's Kitchen

Details help readers "see" the kitchen.

My special place is Aunt Maya's kitchen. It is bright yellow with many plants in baskets. I go there on Saturdays after soccer practice. For lunch I always sit at the round wooden table.

Writer tells what they do.

Sometimes we water the plants or make gingerbread cookies.

Ending tells why the place is special for the writer.

This place is special because it is just for Aunt Maya and me.

Subjects

> The **subject** of a sentence tells who or what does something.
>
> **Neil Armstrong** walked on the moon.
> **The moon** goes around the Earth.

A **Write** each sentence. **Underline** the subject.

1. Ann traveled in an airplane.

2. The airplane flew very high.

3. The girl loved the ride.

4. She will be an astronaut one day.

5. Astronauts study space.

6. One spaceship went to the moon.

7. Men flew in the spaceship.

8. Men and women will go to Mars someday.

B **Choose** a subject from the box to complete each sentence. **Write** the sentences.

The moon	Their homes	Tools
Windows	Some astronauts	

1. ____ fly to a space station.
2. ____ help them work.
3. ____ let them see outside.
4. ____ shines outside their windows.
5. ____ are far away.

C **Write** a subject to complete each sentence. **Check** that your sentences make sense.

6. ____ likes planets.
7. ____ will be an explorer.
8. ____ might fly into space.
9. ____ reads many books.
10. ____ learns new things.

Test Preparation

✓ **Write** the letter of the correct answer.

1. ___ went to the
Space Museum.
- ○ **A** Fly
- ○ **B** David and Stu
- ○ **C** Let

2. ___ were everywhere.
- ○ **A** Play
- ○ **B** Drive
- ○ **C** Airplanes

3. ___ learned about
the planets.
- ○ **A** They
- ○ **B** Far
- ○ **C** Big

4. ___ is as big as Earth.
- ○ **A** Soft
- ○ **B** Blue
- ○ **C** Venus

5. ___ were in the
museum.
- ○ **A** Some children
- ○ **B** Eat
- ○ **C** Stay

6. ___ talked to David.
- ○ **A** Good
- ○ **B** One girl
- ○ **C** Little

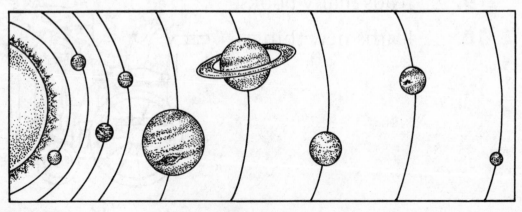

Review

✓ **Write** each sentence. **Underline** the subject.

1. Mark studied about plants in school.

2. The class had a little garden.

3. Plants are interesting.

4. The seeds grow fast.

5. The space station has some plants.

6. Sunlight comes through the windows.

✓ **Choose** the correct subject in ( ). **Write** the sentences.

7. ___ shows things far away. (A telescope, Many)
8. ___ study the sky. (Two men, Fly)
9. ___ is the time for stars. (Sixty, Night)
10. ___ are tiny spots in the sky. (Planets, Pull)
11. ___ looks very close. (See, The moon)
12. ___ is far away. (It, Go)

Use Descriptive Words in Subjects

Use descriptive words in subjects. These words can give readers a clear picture of your subjects.

No Descriptive Words   The rocket was ready.

Descriptive Words   The <u>huge silver</u> rocket was ready.

 Which sentence in each pair gives a clearer picture of the subject? **Write** the sentence.

1. The astronauts walk in space.
   The brave astronauts walk in space.

2. Their bulky spacesuits keep them warm.
   Their spacesuits keep them warm.

3. The happy crew comes home.
   The crew comes home.

4. The proud captain lands the spaceship.
   The captain lands the spaceship.

5. The trip is over.
   The long trip into space is over.

 Write some sentences about the sky at night. **Use** descriptive words in your subjects to give a clear picture.

Make a List

> **Writing Prompt** An astronaut is going on a trip to the moon. Make a list of things she needs for the trip. Tell why she needs those things.

List uses bullets to organize items.

Descriptive words give readers a clear picture of subjects.

Writer explains why the spaceship, spacesuit, and helmet are necessary.

Things an Astronaut Needs

- A fast spaceship takes astronauts.
  The moon is far away.
- A thick spacesuit keeps her warm.
  The moon is a cold place.
- A hard helmet protects her head.
  The moon is a dangerous place.
- Air, water, and food are very important. People need these things to live.
- Other astronauts must go on the trip. There are many jobs to do.

Predicates

The **predicate** tells what the subject of a sentence does or is.

My family **goes on hikes**.
A hike **is fun**.

A **Write** each sentence. **Underline** the predicate.

1. Our family hiked up a mountain.

2. The trail was hard.

3. Dad and I climbed very high.

4. I got very tired.

5. My dad helped me a little.

6. He gave me some water.

7. The view was great.

8. The ground looked far away.

9. Everyone climbed down slowly.

10. The whole family sits and rests.

B **Choose** the predicate that completes each sentence. **Write** the sentence.

1. Lucy (has a backpack, a heavy load).

2. The backpack (to school, is red).

3. Two books (on the bottom, sit inside).

4. One book (tells about a hike, a picture on the cover).

5. Lucy and Mom (a long trip, hike and camp).

C **Choose** a predicate from the box to complete each sentence. **Write** the sentences.

> chattered and ran past us
>
> walked in the woods
>
> grew everywhere
>
> was long
>
> sang in the trees

6. Our family ___.

7. Tall trees ___.

8. A squirrel ___.

9. Birds ___.

10. Our walk ___.

Test Preparation

☑ **Write** the letter of the correct answer.

1. A fawn ___.

  ○ **A** and its mother

  ○ **B** with spots

  ○ **C** is a baby deer

2. The fawn ___.

  ○ **A** long legs

  ○ **B** hides in the grass

  ○ **C** small and brown

3. A baby bear ___.

  ○ **A** is a cub

  ○ **B** with fur

  ○ **C** up a tree

4. Cubs ___.

  ○ **A** brown or black

  ○ **B** sharp teeth

  ○ **C** climb trees and swim

5. A baby fox ___.

  ○ **A** fast

  ○ **B** is a kit

  ○ **C** with red fur

6. A kit ___.

  ○ **A** sleeps in a den

  ○ **B** long nose

  ○ **C** and its mother

Review

✓ **Write** each sentence. **Underline** the predicate.

   1. I saw a rainbow.

   2. It was in the sky.

   3. We stopped and counted the colors.

   4. The rainbow had seven colors.

   5. Dana liked orange best.

   6. The rainbow lasted a long time.

✓ **Choose** the predicate that completes each sentence. **Write** the sentences.

   7. Pedro (has a pet dog, a great pet).

   8. Spot (a cute name, is the dog's name).

   9. This pet (has brown fur, Pedro's friend).

   10. The dog (shakes hands, a trick).

   11. He (good dog, rolls over too).

   12. Pedro and Spot (friends, play together).

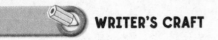

Use Descriptive Words in Predicates

Use descriptive words in predicates. These words can tell more about what happened.

No Descriptive Words   Mudge has a toy.

Descriptive Words   Mudge has a <u>chewy</u> toy <u>in his mouth</u>.

 Which sentence in each pair tells more about what happened? **Write** the sentence.

1. Henry swam.
   Henry swam in the lake.

2. They made a huge fire on the sand.
   They made a fire.

3. Dad cooked dinner.
   Dad cooked fish and potatoes for dinner.

4. Mom set up our new tent under a tree.
   Mom set up our tent.

5. Henry gathered chunks of dry wood.
   Henry gathered wood.

 Write about something you do outdoors. **Use** descriptive words to show readers what happened.

Write an Outdoor Story

> **Writing Prompt** Write a story about an outdoor place that you like. Tell about something that happened there.

Opening sentence tells who, what, when, and where.

Story has a beginning, middle, and end.

Descriptive words tell readers exactly what happened.

Saturday in the Park with Mom

Last Saturday my mom and I went to Thompson Park for a picnic. We sat under a shady oak tree. We put our fruit and sandwiches out on an old wool blanket. Then a squirrel ran over and started looking at our food. We gave him a few ripe cherries. Soon there were six gray squirrels begging for food! Our picnic basket was empty when we went home.

Statements and Questions

A **statement** is a sentence that tells something. A statement ends with a **period (.)**.

Some places are very dry.

A **question** is a sentence that asks something. A question ends with a **question mark (?)**.

Is a desert a dry place?

All statements and questions begin with capital letters.

A **Read** each sentence. **Write** *S* if the sentence is a statement. **Write** *Q* if the sentence is a question.

1. Can an oak tree live in a desert? Q

2. An oak tree needs plenty of water. S

3. It cannot live in a very dry place. S

4. Are there any trees in the desert? Q

5. Where does a cactus grow? Q

6. A cactus can grow in the desert. S

7. Does a cactus have spines? Q

6. A cactus has waxy skin. S

B **Write** the correct statement or question in each pair.

1. (Rattlesnakes live in the desert.)

    rattlesnakes live in the desert

2. I have never seen a rattlesnake?

    (I have never seen a rattlesnake.)

3. (Are they dangerous?)

    are they dangerous?

4. What other animals are in the desert.

    (What other animals are in the desert?)

5. it is too hot for most animals

    (It is too hot for most animals.)

C **Write** the sentences. **Use** a capital letter and the correct end mark.

6. many countries have deserts

7. are the deserts large or small

8. some are very large

9. they are hundreds of miles wide

10. would you like to visit a desert

Test Preparation

✓ **Write** the letter of the correct answer.

1. ○ **A** is a cactus a plant or an animal
   ○ **B** is a cactus a plant or an animal?
   ○ **C** Is a cactus a plant or an animal?

2. ○ **A** A cactus is a plant.
   ○ **B** a cactus is a plant
   ○ **C** A cactus is a plant

3. ○ **A** Do cactuses grow tall
   ○ **B** Do cactuses grow tall?
   ○ **C** do cactuses grow tall

4. ○ **A** Some cactuses are very big
   ○ **B** Some cactuses are very big.
   ○ **C** Some cactuses are very big?

5. ○ **A** Does a cactus have leaves.
   ○ **B** does a cactus have leaves?
   ○ **C** Does a cactus have leaves?

6. ○ **A** A cactus has spines.
   ○ **B** A cactus has spines
   ○ **C** A cactus has spines?

Review

✓ **Write** the sentences. **Circle** each statement. **Underline** each question.

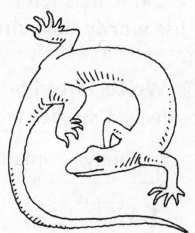

1. Did you go to the desert?

2. We went for a visit.

3. I rode a mule.

4. Did you see a lizard?

5. We saw one lizard.

6. Will you go back?

✓ **Write** each sentence correctly. **Use** a capital letter and the correct end mark.

7. some birds live in the desert

8. which birds live there

9. you can find woodpeckers in deserts

10. hawks also live in the desert

11. some birds build nests in cactuses

12. what kinds of birds do that

Words That Show Feelings

Good writers tell how they feel. They use **words that show their feelings**.

 Write a word from the box to tell how the writer feels. **Use** each word one time.

happy	mad	tired	sad	scared

1. We feel ___. Our dog is lost.

2. The boy is ___. He sees a tornado.

3. Sara is ___. She won first prize.

4. I am ___. Linda took the last apple.

5. Juan feels ___. He just ran eight miles.

 Write about something you did for the first time. **Use** words that show how you felt.

Tell About Your Neighborhood

Writing Prompt Write about your neighborhood. Tell what happens there and how you feel about it.

Writer begins with main idea about her neighborhood.

Details support the main idea and help readers "see" and "hear" the place.

Writer tells how she feels about topic.

A Busy Neighborhood

My neighborhood is a busy place. Cars, trucks, and buses rush up and down. Horns honk and sirens scream. Big machines fix holes in the streets. People hurry in and out of the stores and buildings. They talk and laugh and shout. My neighborhood is busy, but it is also exciting. I love it because something is always going on there.

Commands and Exclamations

A **command** is a sentence that tells someone to do something. It ends with a **period (.)**. The subject of a command is *you*, but *you* is usually not shown.

> Pack your suitcase.   Please come with me.

An **exclamation** is a sentence that shows surprise or strong feelings. It ends with an **exclamation mark (!)**.

> What a great trip this will be!   I am so happy!

All commands and exclamations begin with capital letters.

A **Write** each sentence. **Write** C if the sentence is a command. **Write** E if it is an exclamation.

1. Bring your camera. C
2. Put your jacket on. C
3. Oh dear, we are so late! e
4. Please get in the car. C
5. Hooray, we're on our way! e

B **Write** the correct command or exclamation in each pair.

1. My, what a lot of snow there is!
   My, what a lot of snow there is.

2. play in the snow with me.
   Play in the snow with me.

3. Please put on your mittens?
   Please put on your mittens.

4. here comes the sun?
   Here comes the sun!

5. Oh no, the snow is gone?
   Oh no, the snow is gone!

C **Complete** each command or exclamation. **Put** a period at the end if the sentence is a command. **Put** an exclamation mark at the end if the sentence is an exclamation.

6. Look at this ___

7. Wow, it ___

8. How beautiful ___

9. Take a ___

10. Show everyone ___

Test Preparation

✓ **Write** the letter of the correct answer.

1. ○ **A** pick up this rock
   ✓ **B** Pick up this rock.
   ○ **C** Pick up this rock

2. ✓ **A** It is so heavy!
   ○ **B** it is so heavy.
   ○ **C** It is so heavy

3. ○ **A** please be careful?
   ○ **B** Please be careful
   ✓ **C** Please be careful.

4. ✓ **A** I have a great idea!
   ○ **B** i have a great idea!
   ○ **C** I have a great idea

5. ○ **A** Stand over there
   ✓ **B** Stand over there.
   ○ **C** stand over there!

6. ○ **A** hurray, we did it
   ○ **B** hurray, we did it.
   ✓ **C** Hurray, we did it!

Review

✓ **Write** the sentences. **Circle** each command.
Underline each exclamation.

1. Please help me.

2. Choose the strongest animal.

3. Gosh, that is hard!

4. Tell me your answer.

5. I just don't know!

6. Make your best guess.

✓ **Write** each sentence correctly. **Use** a capital letter
and the correct end mark.

7. look at this ant

8. wow, it is so tiny

9. what a huge crumb it has

10. pick up your lunch

11. ants are on my sandwich

12. throw it away

Use Commands and Exclamations

> **Use commands and exclamations** to add variety to your sentences. They also let your readers know your feelings.
>
> Look at those ants. How tiny they are!

 Which sentence in each pair shows strong feelings? **Write** the sentence.

1. We saw many ants.
   We had never seen so many ants!

2. That ant bit me!
   Do ants bite?

3. Don't step on the ants.
   The ants are on the steps.

4. The ants are moving slowly.
   Watch the ants carry those big crumbs.

5. I think ants are amazing!
   Do you like ants?

 Write about something exciting that happened to you. **Use** a command and an exclamation.

Tell a Tale About an Animal

Writing Prompt Imagine that you have discovered an amazing animal. Tell what the animal is and why it is amazing. Also tell how you feel about the discovery.

Writer mixes real and make-believe details.

Writer shows his feelings.

Writer ends with a command.

A Talking Rabbit!

Yesterday I was walking home from school. As I passed by the woods near the highway, I heard someone say hello. I looked around, but no one was there. Then I saw a rabbit. It told me its name was Roger. I had found a talking rabbit! I was so excited! I asked Roger to come with me. Look for us tonight on the news.

Nouns

A **noun** names a person, place, animal, or thing.

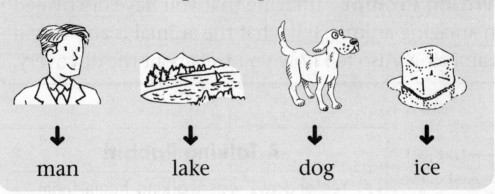

man   lake   dog   ice

A **Write** the noun in each sentence. **Write** *person, place, animal,* or *thing* to tell what the noun names.

1. The boy was waiting.

2. His farm is nearby.

3. Chickens cluck noisily.

4. The barn is large and red.

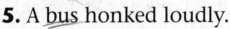

5. A bus honked loudly.

6. A child waved.

7. The park is far.

8. The dog barks.

B There are three nouns in each sentence. One noun is underlined. **Write** the other two nouns.

1. The pond was covered with <u>ice</u> and snow.

2. The ducks and <u>geese</u> had no food.

3. Two <u>children</u> lived in a house across the street.

4. The girl and boy brought <u>bread</u>.

5. With many loud <u>honks</u>, the birds ate the crumbs.

C **Complete** each sentence with a noun. **Write** the sentences.

6. My dog and I play in the ___.

7. I toss him a ___.

8. My dog may chase a ___.

9. My ___ comes too.

10. The dog runs on the ___.

Test Preparation

☑ **Write** the letter of the correct answer.

1. Dogs are our ___.
   - ○ **A** happy
   - ○ **B** friends
   - ○ **C** soft

2. They can have important ___.
   - ○ **A** run
   - ○ **B** swim
   - ○ **C** jobs

3. Some dogs are ___ for people.
   - ○ **A** few
   - ○ **B** bark
   - ○ **C** helpers

4. Some dogs find people in the ___.
   - ○ **A** woods
   - ○ **B** look
   - ○ **C** right

5. Strong dogs can pull ___.
   - ○ **A** sleds
   - ○ **B** find
   - ○ **C** like

6. A dog may watch a ___.
   - ○ **A** have
   - ○ **B** house
   - ○ **C** new

Review

✓ **Choose** the noun in ( ) to complete each sentence. **Write** the sentences.

    1. There are all kinds of (dogs, says).

    2. Some dogs have short (very, tails).

    3. Many dogs have long (sing, hair).

    4. Most dogs have sharp (keep, teeth).

    5. Some dogs swim in (old, lakes).

    6. Many (know, people) like dogs.

✓ **Choose** a noun from the box to replace each underlined word. **Write** the sentences.

food	vet	dish	yard	dog	tub

    7. A pet <u>animal</u> needs care.

    8. Feed it good <u>thing</u>.

    9. Put food in a <u>thing</u>.

  10. Play in the <u>place</u> with your dog.

  11. Wash your pet in a <u>thing</u>.

  12. Take your dog to a <u>person</u>.

Time-order Words

Good writers use **time-order words** to show readers the order of steps or events. Some time-order words are *first, next, then, later, now, tomorrow,* and *last.*

First I got up. **Next** I brushed my teeth.

Then I got dressed. **Last** I ate breakfast.

 Choose the best order for the sentences. **Find** a word in the Word Bank to begin each sentence. **Write** the sentences in a paragraph.

First	Next	Then	Last

1. ___ Bill opens the door for Turk.

2. ___ Turk brings his leash to Bill.

3. ___ Turk rushes outside.

4. ___ Bill puts the leash on Turk.

 Tell how to make or do something. **Put** your sentences in order. **Use** time-order words.

Write Directions

Writing Prompt Write directions to help a new student get from your classroom to the lunchroom.

Writer tells what directions are for in first sentence.

Writer uses time-order words to show order of steps.

Details make directions clear.

How to Get to the Lunchroom

Follow these directions to get from our classroom to the lunchroom. First go out the classroom door and turn right. Next walk to the end of the hall. You will pass six classrooms and the gym. Then turn left and go down the stairs. Now turn left again. Walk to the second door on the right. Go through that door, and you are in the lunchroom.

Proper Nouns

Proper nouns are special names for people, places, animals, and things. They begin with capital letters. **Days of the week, months of the year,** and **holidays** also begin with capital letters. **Titles** for people begin with capital letters. Many titles end with a **period (.)**. Some proper nouns have more than one word.

Mr. Morgan threw the ball. **Ronald Morgan** swung at it. He got his first hit on **Tuesday, May** 10, in **Walker Park**.

Ⓐ **Write** the two proper nouns in each sentence.

1. Alicia Ortiz broke her arm on July 1.

2. Dr. Lee said not to play baseball until Labor Day.

3. On Friday the girl was back at Pioneer Park.

4. Her team, the Patton Panthers, was playing the Terry Tigers.

5. "Go, Roberto! Come on, Cindy!" she shouted.

6. The next game is at Anders Field on the Fourth of July.

B **Write** the two proper nouns in each sentence correctly. Some proper nouns have more than one word.

1. Our new coach, mrs. alice ray, moved here in june.

2. On monday morning she met us at morgan field.

3. This park is on doyle road, near the town of amber.

4. Our game with the raytown ravens will be on flag day.

5. My friends marcus and leo are great players.

6. Our old coach, mr. franklin, moved to cleveland.

C **Complete** each sentence with a proper noun of your own. The word in ( ) tells you what kind of proper noun to use. **Write** the sentences.

7. I have a friend named ___. (person's name)

8. Our birthdays are in ___. (month)

9. We both like ___. (holiday)

10. We both have pets named ___. (animal's name)

Test Preparation

Write the letter of the correct answer.

1. One baseball team is the ___.

  ○ **A** Chicago cubs
  ○ **B** chicago cubs
  ○ **C** Chicago Cubs

2. There are baseball teams in ___.

  ○ **A** boston and dallas
  ○ **B** Boston and Dallas
  ○ **C** Boston and dallas

3. One famous baseball player was ___.

  ○ **A** Mr. babe ruth
  ○ **B** Mr. Babe Ruth
  ○ **C** mr. Babe Ruth

4. The season ends after ___.

  ○ **A** Labor Day
  ○ **B** Labor day
  ○ **C** labor day

5. The World Series begins in ___.

  ○ **A** october
  ○ **B** OCTOBER
  ○ **C** October

6. ___ want to go to a game.

  ○ **A** Liz and Tom
  ○ **B** Liz and tom
  ○ **C** liz and tom

Review

☑ **Write** the proper nouns in the sentences correctly. The number in ( ) tells how many proper nouns are in the sentence.

1. mrs. smith helps me with math. (1)

2. She also coaches the bayfield bears. (1)

3. I go to her house every monday. (1)

4. It is on maple street next to lincoln school. (2)

5. The smiths have a cat called mr. fluffy. (2)

6. alex smith got the cat in april. (2)

☑ **Complete** each sentence with a proper noun from the box. **Write** the sentences. **Write** the proper nouns correctly.

ms. brown	labor day
atlantic ocean	florida

7. Ben lives in the state of ___.

8. He swims in the ___.

9. ___ is teaching him.

10. By ___, he will swim well.

Use Precise Nouns

Use **precise nouns** in your writing.
Precise nouns give your readers clear pictures.

Those <u>people</u> are the <u>team</u>.

↓   ↓

Those <u>players</u> are the <u>Midville</u> <u>Mavericks</u>.

 Choose a noun from the box to replace the underlined words in each sentence. **Write** the sentences.

uniforms	gloves	dugout
Dave Wilson	Riverside Field	

1. The Mavericks play at <u>the park</u>.

2. They wear <u>clothes</u> with red stripes.

3. <u>That man</u> is their best pitcher.

4. The players sit in the <u>place</u>.

5. They carry their <u>things</u> onto the field.

 Write a paragraph about a game or activity.
Use precise nouns to make a clear picture.

Tell How to Pick a Fantasy Team

Writing Prompt   Imagine you are picking players for a baseball team. The players on this fantasy team must be animals. Choose several animals, and tell why they can or cannot be on your team.

First sentence tells what the paragraph is about.

Writer uses exact nouns to make a clear picture.

Ending is funny.

A Fantasy Team

What animals would I choose to play on my fantasy baseball team? An octopus can throw, catch, and hit, but it cannot run. A horse cannot throw, catch, or hit, but it can run. The octopus could be the pitcher. The horse could run in place of the octopus. Monkeys would make good players. They can run, hit, catch, and throw. They could play on the bases and in the field. Fish would be terrible players. They cannot run, hit, catch, or throw!

Singular and Plural Nouns

A **singular noun** names one person, place, animal, or thing. A noun that names more than one is called a **plural noun**.

turtle (one)   bears (more than one)

You add **-s** to most nouns to show more than one. If a noun ends in **s, ch, sh,** or **x,** add **-es** to the noun to show more than one.

rabbits (add **-s**)   foxes (add **-es**)

A **Add** -s or -es to each singular noun. **Write** the plural noun.

1. tree

2. bus

3. shoe

4. box

5. lamp

6. dish

B **Write** each sentence. **Underline** the singular noun. **Circle** the plural noun.

    1. A rabbit raced with turtles.

    2. Only one raccoon watched from the benches.

    3. The squirrels rested under a tree.

    4. The cow was eating some tall grasses.

    5. The race had no winners.

    6. The animals gave up and had a party.

C **Add** *-s* or *-es* to each word in ( ). **Write** the sentences.

    7. The (bear) were not happy.

    8. Some (branch) fell into the stream.

    9. Two (beaver) helped.

    10. They chewed the wood into (piece).

    11. (Fox) pulled the wood from the stream.

    12. The rabbits under the (bush) were glad.

Test Preparation

✓ **Write** the letter of the correct answer.

1. In a story, ___ may do silly things.

    ○ **A** animalz
    ○ **B** animals
    ○ **C** animales

2. A turtle may make some ___.

    ○ **A** sandwich
    ○ **B** sandwichs
    ○ **C** sandwiches

3. Squirrels may wrap ___ of nuts.

    ○ **A** boxses
    ○ **B** boxss
    ○ **C** boxes

4. One ___ sings silly songs.

    ○ **A** chipmunk
    ○ **B** chipmunks
    ○ **C** chipmunkes

5. Beavers might ride in ___.

    ○ **A** busez
    ○ **B** buses
    ○ **C** buss

6. Bears might paint with ___.

    ○ **A** brushes
    ○ **B** brush
    ○ **C** brushs

Review

☑ **Add** -s or -es to each singular noun. **Write** the plural noun.

1. stick
2. lunch
3. bus
4. bird

5. bush
6. rock
7. mailbox
8. dish

☑ **Choose** the correct noun in ( ). **Write** the sentences.

9. Turtle stood on a (rock, rocks).

10. He made (speechs, speeches) there.

11. Squirrels peeked out of (bushs, bushes).

12. (Foxes, Foxs) sat on logs.

13. The (rabbits, rabbites) listened too.

14. They were hiding in the (ditchs, ditches).

Organization

Before you write, think about how you will **organize** your ideas. Here are some ways you can organize.

- Use time-order words such as *first*, *next*, *then*, *later*, *now*, and *last*.
- Put your ideas in a list, diagram, or chart.

 Write the sentences in the correct order to tell what happened.

1. Next, we looked for facts in the library.

2. First, Beth and I chose butterflies for our topic.

3. Then we wrote a draft of our report.

 Add a time-order word to each sentence. **Write** the sentences in the correct order.

4. ___ I painted the picture.

5. ___, I got my paints and white paper.

 Make a plan for what you will do next weekend. **Use** a chart to help you organize your writing.

Write a Plan

Writing Prompt Imagine you have to share a room with Alex. Alex is very different from you. Write a plan. Tell what you can do to help you get along with Alex.

Writer uses a list to organize his ideas. A bullet marks each point.

Writer begins each point with statement of an idea.

Writer gives details that explain his ideas.

My Plan

- I will not get angry. If Alex leaves his clothes on my side of the room, I will not say anything mean.

- I will show Alex what to do. If I keep my side clean, then he may keep his side clean too.

- I will be friendly and polite. I will try to smile at Alex. I will thank him if he cleans up.

Plural Nouns That Change Spelling

A **plural noun** names more than one person, place, animal, or thing. Some nouns change spelling to name more than one.

Singular	Plural	Singular	Plural
child	children	leaf	leaves
man	men	wolf	wolves
woman	women	mouse	mice
tooth	teeth	goose	geese
foot	feet		

A **Write** the plural noun for each singular noun.

1. tooth

2. child

3. foot

4. mouse

5. woman

6. leaf

B **Choose** the correct noun in ( ) to complete each sentence. **Write** the sentences.

1. What sound do (gooses, geese) make?

2. A goose has flat (feet, foots).

3. What sound do (mice, mouses) make?

4. A mouse has sharp (tooths, teeth).

5. What sounds do (childs, children) make?

6. How many shoes do two (mans, men) need?

C **Change** the noun in ( ) to a plural noun. **Write** the question. **Write** an answer to the question.

Example   How are (wolf) like the wind?
How are wolves like the wind?
Wolves and the wind howl.

7. How are (goose) like car horns?

8. How are (foot) like socks?

9. How are (tooth) like pins?

10. How are (leaf) like snowflakes?

Test Preparation

✓ **Write** the letter of the correct answer.

1. Three ___ listened for sounds.

- ○ **A** children
- ○ **B** child
- ○ **C** childs

2. They heard many ___ honking.

- ○ **A** gooses
- ○ **B** geese
- ○ **C** goose

3. Horses were stamping their ___.

- ○ **A** feets
- ○ **B** foots
- ○ **C** feet

4. Some ___ fed clucking hens.

- ○ **A** womans
- ○ **B** women
- ○ **C** womens

5. A family of ___ squeaked in the barn.

- ○ **A** mices
- ○ **B** mouses
- ○ **C** mice

6. Four ___ milked mooing cows.

- ○ **A** men
- ○ **B** mans
- ○ **C** mens

Review

✓ **Choose** the correct noun in ( ) to complete each sentence. **Write** the noun.

1. The (mouses, mice) were fine musicians.

2. The (childs, children) clapped to the beat.

3. They tapped their (feet, foots).

4. The (geese, gooses) honked the tune.

5. The donkey smiled and showed his (tooths, teeth).

6. Many (womans, women) came for the concert.

✓ **Change** each noun in ( ) to a plural noun. **Write** the sentences.

7. Two ___ have a big barn. (man)

8. They care for sick ___. (goose)

9. That runner has sore ___. (foot)

10. The old dog has few ___. (tooth)

11. Many tiny ___ find a home. (mouse)

12. ___ help with the animals. (child)

Put Ideas in Order

One way to **put ideas in order** is to use time order. Here are two more ways.

- Use **space order.** Tell about something from top to bottom or from left to right.

- Use **compare and contrast order.** Tell how things are alike. Tell how they are different.

 Read each paragraph. **Write** the letter of the order of the ideas in the paragraph.

    A   space order
    B   compare and contrast order

1. Vince and Joe have dark hair and brown eyes. They are both good at math. Vince likes movies. He wants to be an actor. Joe likes books. He wants to be a teacher.

2. Angela arranged her books in her new bookcase. She put sports books on the top shelf. Nature books are on the middle shelf. Mysteries are on the bottom shelf.

 Describe two family members, two books, or two animals. **Use** compare and contrast order.

Make a Poster

> **Writing Prompt**   Think about how you would form a book club. Make a poster to tell people how they can form a book club.

Title tells the topic of the poster.

The writer spells plural nouns correctly.

Steps are arranged in order.

How to Form a Book Club

1. Find other children who like to read. Ask your friends, and have them ask their friends.

2. Choose a place to meet. Your home could be the first meeting place.

3. Pick a date and time for the meeting.

4. Vote on a book for everyone to read.

5. Meet and talk about the book.

Possessive Nouns

A noun that shows who or what owns something is a **possessive noun**. To show ownership, add an **apostrophe (')** and **-s** when the noun is singular. Add just an **apostrophe (')** when the noun is plural.

the turkey's wings

rabbits' tails

A **Add** *'s* to each singular noun in ( ).
Write the words.

1. the (horse) head

2. the (goat) legs

3. the (bear) fur

Add *'* to each plural noun in ( ).
Write the words.

4. the (monkeys) tails

5. the (giraffes) necks

6. the (birds) wings

B Write the possessive noun in ( ) to complete each sentence.

1. Watch out for a (porcupines, porcupine's) quills.

2. All the (quill's, quills') tips are sharp.

3. The quills stick to an (attacker, attacker's) body.

4. We pulled quills out of our (dogs, dogs') noses.

5. They stay away from that (animal's, animals') home!

6. Do (skunk, skunks') odors protect them too?

C Rewrite each sentence. **Use** 's or ' to write the underlined words as a possessive noun.

7. We had Thanksgiving dinner at <u>the house of our neighbors</u>.

8. Mr. Brown wore his <u>outfit of a Pilgrim</u>.

9. Mrs. Brown made <u>the cake of her grandmother</u>.

10. The turkey came from <u>the yard of a farmer</u>.

11. Dad liked the <u>taste of yams</u>.

12. The pumpkin pie was <u>the favorite of Mom</u>.

Test Preparation

✓ **Write** the letter of the correct answer.

1. The two ___ plan was great!
   - ○ **A** rabbit
   - ○ **B** rabbits'
   - ○ **C** rabbit's

2. They had a party for ___ birthday.
   - ○ **A** Moose
   - ○ **B** Moose'
   - ○ **C** Moose's

3. The ___ surprise was a big cake.
   - ○ **A** friends'
   - ○ **B** friends
   - ○ **C** friend

4. The ___ top had 18 candles.
   - ○ **A** cake
   - ○ **B** cakes'
   - ○ **C** cake's

5. All the ___ flames glowed brightly.
   - ○ **A** candles'
   - ○ **B** candle'
   - ○ **C** candle's

6. The ___ party surprised Moose.
   - ○ **A** animals
   - ○ **B** animals'
   - ○ **C** animals's

Review

✔ **Add** 's or ' to each word in ( ). **Write** the sentences.

1. Cheese can be made from a (goat) milk.

2. A (sheep) wool is made into yarn.

3. You can boil, fry, or scramble (hens) eggs.

4. (Bees) honey tastes great on toast.

5. A (cow) milk can make you healthy.

6. (Ostriches) eggs can feed many people.

✔ **Choose** the word in ( ) that completes each sentence. **Write** the sentences.

7. One (turkey's, turkeys') feathers are black.

8. Most (turkey's, turkeys') feathers are white.

9. Three (kittens', kitten's) fur is white.

10. One (kittens', kitten's) fur is brown.

11. Many (goat's, goats') hair is long.

12. That (goat's, goats') hair is short.

13. Your (cat's, cats') tail is bushy.

14. Those two (dog's, dogs') tails are wagging.

Include All the Information

Writers should **include all the information** that readers need to know. In an invitation, include the date, time, and place. In a note, include whom the note is for, whom it is from, and what it is about.

Read the invitation and the note below.
Write the missing information.

> _____**Lucy Hall**_____ **Is Having a Party!**
>
> **For** Valentine's Day_____
>
> **Date**_____
>
> **Time**_____
>
> **Place** 3431 Third Street_____

To Mom
From
Wants to change Tuesday appointment to Thursday. Call him at 616-555-3678.
Message taken by

Write a note inviting a friend to do something.
Include all the information.

Write an Invitation

Writing Prompt Your class is giving a party. Write an invitation asking other people at your school to come. Be sure to include all the information that the people need to know.

Come to Our Party!

Purpose of party is given in first sentence.

The students in Mrs. McAvie's second grade class are having a Thanksgiving party. You are invited! The party is on Wednesday, November 20, at 2:30 P.M. in Room 105. Dress up like a Pilgrim if you like. There will be pumpkin cookies, orange punch, and games. Please let us know if you can come.

Writer gives information that readers need to know in second sentence.

Additional details are given in later sentences.

Verbs

A word that shows action is a **verb**.

Ahmed **makes** a present for his dad.

The word **makes** is a verb. It tells what Ahmed does.

A **Write** the verb in each sentence.

1. Ahmed finds a small flat piece of wood.

2. He sands the wood.

3. Next Ahmed cuts the edges.

4. He picks his dad's favorite color.

5. Ahmed paints the wood yellow.

6. He prints "The Best Dad" in black.

7. Then he wraps the gift.

8. Ahmed's dad opens the present.

9. Dad thanks Ahmed.

10. Dad and Ahmed hug each other.

B Add a word in ( ) to each sentence.
Write the sentences.

  1. Henry (buys, plays) two plants.

  2. He (wears, puts) one plant in the sun.

  3. He (sets, tells) one plant in the dark.

  4. One plant (sleeps, grows) tall.

  5. One plant (dies, makes).

  6. Plants (need, cut) light.

C Write a verb from the box to complete
each sentence.

kicks	paints	hums
writes	builds	bakes

  7. Lucy ___ a story at school.

  8. Walter ___ pictures.

  9. Henry ___ happy tunes.

  10. Maria ___ a pie.

  11. Ling ___ a football.

  12. Ann ___ a robot.

Test Preparation

✓ **Write** the letter of the correct answer.

1. An ant ___ on six legs.
   - ○ **A** bug
   - ○ **B** walks
   - ○ **C** feet

2. Some ants ___ in tunnels.
   - ○ **A** tiny
   - ○ **B** dirt
   - ○ **C** live

3. Ants ___ in long lines.
   - ○ **A** red
   - ○ **B** surprise
   - ○ **C** march

4. A queen ant ___ many eggs.
   - ○ **A** lays
   - ○ **B** round
   - ○ **C** small

5. A worker ant ___ for food.
   - ○ **A** busy
   - ○ **B** looks
   - ○ **C** good

6. An ant ___ heavy things.
   - ○ **A** lifts
   - ○ **B** hill
   - ○ **C** big

Review

✓ **Write** each sentence. **Underline** the verb.

1. Bess and Ella pick a science project.

2. They build a robot dog.

3. The robot dog barks.

4. It hops into the air.

5. The dog wags its metal tail.

6. The girls win a prize at the science fair.

✓ **Complete** each sentence with a word in ( ). **Write** the sentences.

7. Andy (makes, helps) a baked potato.

8. He (glues, washes) the potato.

9. He (sends, pokes) holes in it with a fork.

10. He and Mom (wrap, stop) the potato in foil.

11. They (think, bake) the potato in the oven.

12. Then Andy (draws, eats) the potato.

Strong Verbs

Use **strong verbs**. They give readers a clear picture of exactly what is happening.

Weak Verb   Sara <u>gets</u> red beads.

Strong Verb   Sara <u>buys</u> red beads.

 Replace the underlined verb with a strong verb from the box. **Write** the new sentences.

declares	race	squeeze	builds	carry

1. On Saturday the girls <u>walk</u> over to Sara's house.

2. Each girl <u>makes</u> part of a model castle.

3. The girls <u>take</u> the model to the backyard.

4. They <u>go</u> through a tight doorway.

5. Sara <u>says</u> our model is the best ever.

 Write about something you have made. **Use** strong verbs.

Make a Robot

Writing Prompt   Imagine that you are creating a robot for a science project. Write a plan for your robot. Tell what it looks like, how it moves, and what it can do.

First sentence shows that plan will focus on the robot.

Writer uses strong verbs to describe robot's actions.

Best of all signals most important thing robot will do.

My Robot

My robot will look like me, with brown eyes and black hair. It will walk and run like me, so it can go to school and play games with me. It will carry my backpack. My robot will obey only me. Best of all, it will help me do my homework. But my robot won't talk, laugh, or smile like I do. I don't want it to be too much like me!

Verbs with Singular and Plural Nouns

Add **-s** to a verb to tell what one person, animal, or thing does. Do **not** add **-s** to a verb that tells what two or more people, animals, or things do.

One child **draws** a car.

Two children **draw** flowers.

Lulu and Pedro **draw** a house.

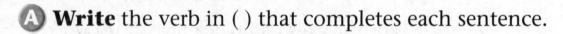

A **Write** the verb in ( ) that completes each sentence.

1. The children (paints, paint) a big picture.

2. One girl (makes, make) a road.

3. Two boys (adds, add) cars and trucks.

4. Three girls (colors, color) the sky blue.

5. Al (uses, use) yellow for a sun.

6. The teacher (hangs, hang) the picture on the wall.

7. The picture (covers, cover) the whole wall.

8. The students (loves, love) their beautiful picture.

B **Write** the verb in ( ) if it is correct. **Change** the verb if it is not correct. **Add** -s.

1. Juno and his mom (walk) to the mailbox.

2. Many letters (sit) inside the box.

3. Juno (take) out the mail.

4. Mom (hope) one letter is for her.

5. A letter (come) for Juno.

6. Mom and Dad (get) five bills.

C **Choose** a verb from the box to complete each sentence. **Add** -s to the verb if the subject is one person or thing. **Write** the sentence.

peek	soar	hug	land	drift	stare

7. A plane ___ through the sky.

8. Jenny ___ out a window.

9. Clouds ___ past.

10. She ___ at tiny houses below.

11. The plane ___ at the airport.

12. Grandma and Grandpa ___ Jenny.

Test Preparation

✓ **Write** the letter of the correct answer.

1. Pedro ___ pictures with a camera.

  ○ **A** fold
  ○ **B** takes
  ○ **C** take

2. Some pictures ___ his dog.

  ○ **A** shows
  ○ **B** show
  ○ **C** colors

3. Three pictures ___ too dark.

  ○ **A** look
  ○ **B** looks
  ○ **C** opens

4. The boy ___ some pictures in a book.

  ○ **A** read
  ○ **B** glue
  ○ **C** glues

5. Rosa and Ida ___ two pictures

  ○ **A** meets
  ○ **B** gets
  ○ **C** get

6. The girls ___ the pictures.

  ○ **A** like
  ○ **B** likes
  ○ **C** pins

Review

✓ **Choose** the verb in ( ) that completes each sentence. **Write** the sentences.

1. My grandma (live, lives) in Korea.

2. Aunt Keiko (write, writes) to her.

3. Two cousins (visit, visits) us.

4. Mom (call, calls) her sister in China.

5. My uncles (teach, teaches) in California.

6. Grandpa (lose, loses) his pictures of Japan.

✓ **Write** the verb in ( ) if it is correct. **Change** the verb if it is not correct. **Add** -*s*.

7. Ling (draw) many pictures.

8. Some pictures (show) Ling with her flute.

9. Dad and Ling (find) magnets.

10. A magnet (stick) to metal.

11. One picture (hang) on the door.

12. Mom (give) Ling a hug.

13. Mom (read) her book.

14. They (like) the pictures.

Words That Compare and Contrast

When you **compare,** you tell how things are alike. Use the words *and, like, too,* and *both* to compare things. When you **contrast**, you tell how things are different. Use *but* and *unlike* to contrast things.

Alike   <u>Both</u> Joy and I take dance lessons.

Different   Joy likes ballet, <u>but</u> I like tap.

 Write the word in ( ) that works in each sentence.

1. I like my piano lessons, (but, both) Joy does not like hers.

2. (Both, Unlike) Joy and I practice every day for an hour.

3. Joy begins practicing at 3 o'clock. (Like, Unlike) her, I begin at 2 o'clock.

4. My teacher is Mr. Nathan. He teaches Joy (and, too).

 Write about you and a friend. **Tell** how you are alike and different.

Compare Two Animals

Writing Prompt   Choose two animals. Compare the ways these animals communicate. How are they alike? How are they different?

Writer uses *Both* to signal ways the animals are alike.

Writer first tells how cats and dogs are alike and then tells how they are different.

Animal Talk

Both cats and dogs use sounds to tell you things. Cats hiss and dogs growl when they are angry. Cats meow and dogs bark when they want something.

Cats and dogs do different things to let you know how they feel. Cats fluff their tails when they are scared. Dogs wag their tails when they are happy.

Writer uses *but* to show a difference.

Most animals like to be petted. Dogs nudge you with a paw to ask for love. Cats like to be petted too, but they may not beg you.

Verbs for Present, Past, and Future

Today Jeb **bakes** muffins.

The verb **bakes** tells about now. It ends with **-s**.

Yesterday Jeb **baked** muffins.

The verb **baked** tells about the past. It ends with **-ed**.

Tomorrow Jeb **will bake** muffins.

The verb **will bake** tells about the future. It begins with **will**.

A **Write** the verb in each sentence.
Write N if the verb tells about now. **Write** P if the verb tells about the past. **Write** F if the verb tells about the future.

1. Jeb makes new kinds of muffins.

2. Today he puts in nuts.

3. Last week he mixed in oranges.

4. Yesterday he added pineapple.

5. Next week he will use squash.

6. In the future, I will cook my own muffins.

B **Add** -s, -ed, or will to the underlined verb. **Follow** the directions in ( ). **Write** the sentences.

1. Last night Travis <u>yawn</u>. (past)

2. Then he <u>climb</u> into bed. (past)

3. Soon Travis <u>take</u> a walk. (future)

4. Now he <u>spot</u> his friend Nixon. (present)

5. Later he meet another friend. (future)

6. Last week all the friends race their bikes. (past)

C **Choose** the verb from the box that completes each sentence. **Add** -s, -ed, or will to each verb. **Write** the sentences.

pick	help	look
want	bake	invite

7. Tomorrow Carmen ___ cherry pies.

8. Yesterday she ___ the cherries.

9. Chiyo ___ Carmen with that job.

10. Today Carmen ___ her friends for dinner.

11. Artie ___ pie right now!

12. Next week Carmen ___ for more cherries.

Test Preparation

✓ **Write** the letter that tells the time of the verb.

1. Yesterday Leroy watched a spider.

- ○ **A** now
- ○ **B** past
- ○ **C** future

2. The spider's web looks beautiful.

- ○ **A** now
- ○ **B** past
- ○ **C** future

3. Then Leroy checked the spider web.

- ○ **A** now
- ○ **B** past
- ○ **C** future

4. The spider will run away from him.

- ○ **A** now
- ○ **B** past
- ○ **C** future

5. Maybe later the spider will stay.

- ○ **A** now
- ○ **B** past
- ○ **C** future

6. Now Leroy visits the web again.

- ○ **A** now
- ○ **B** past
- ○ **C** future

Review

✓ **Write** the sentences. **Underline** the verb in each sentence. **Write** *N* if the verb tells about now. **Write** *P* if the verb tells about the past. **Write** *F* if the verb tells about the future.

1. Last week Ted fished.
2. Next week he will play soccer.
3. Right now he helps his sister.
4. He reads to her.
5. Later he will wash dishes.
6. Yesterday he cleaned his room.

✓ **Choose** the correct verb in ( ) for each sentence. **Write** the sentences.

7. Yesterday we (laughed, will laugh) at a funny story.
8. Now we (listen, listened) to a new story.
9. Tomorrow we (visited, will visit) the library.
10. I (picked, will pick) an animal book there.

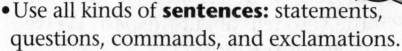

Use Different Sentences

- Use all kinds of **sentences:** statements, questions, commands, and exclamations.
- Use different beginnings. Don't start too many sentences with *the, he, she, it,* or *I.*

Write what kind of sentence each one is: *statement, question, command,* or *exclamation.*

1. That is an amazing car! **2.** Tell me about it. **3.** How fast can it go? **4.** Someday I want a car like that.

Rearrange the words in each sentence so that it begins with the underlined words. **Write** the new sentences.

I look at paintings by a different artist <u>each time</u>. I looked at paintings by Monet <u>last week</u>. I will see paintings by Picasso <u>next time</u>.

Write about two things you have done in the last week. **Use** a command and an exclamation. **Begin** each sentence with a different word.

Write Advice

Writing Prompt What does it mean to be a good friend? Write advice about what a good friend does and does not do.

Good Friends

Writer begins each paragraph with a question and then answers it.

First paragraph tells things that good friends do.

What do good friends do? Good friends listen to what you say. They laugh at your jokes. They share their food and toys with you. You can borrow their things because they trust you.

Second paragraph tells things that good friends do not do.

What do good friends not do? Good friends don't tell your secrets. They don't make fun of you, and they don't lie to you. They never pick you last for a team because you are always first with them.

Writer uses different kinds of sentences.

Keep your good friends. They are a great treasure!

More About Verbs

Use the correct verb in each sentence to show something happening now, in the past, or in the future.

Today Chris **plays** the piano. (now)
Yesterday Chris **played** the piano.
　　(in the past)
Tomorrow Chris **will play** the piano.
　　(in the future)

A **Write** the sentences. **Use** the verb in ( ) that completes the sentence.

　　1. Chris (started, will start) piano lessons three years ago.

　　2. Now she (practices, practiced) an hour each day.

　　3. Last week her sister (dances, danced) in the school show.

　　4. Today their mother (cooks, cooked) soup for the girls.

　　5. Next year she (takes, will take) them to music camp.

B **Add** -s, -ed, or *will* to each verb in ( ).
Write each sentence.

1. Brad (stir) some corn soup now.

2. Yesterday he (boil) corn on the cob.

3. Tomorrow he (bake) cornbread.

4. Next Saturday he (pop) popcorn.

5. Last week he (fix) corn muffins.

6. Now Brad (think) of more ideas for corn.

C **Complete** each sentence with a verb from the box. **Write** each sentence. **Write** *now, past,* or *future* to tell when the action happened.

invites	will make	will glue
played	calls	picked

7. Last week Blanca and Rosa ___ at the beach.

8. They ___ up shells.

9. Now Blanca ___ Rosa on the phone.

10. She ___ Rosa to a birthday party.

11. Tomorrow Rosa ___ a gift for Blanca.

12. She ___ shells on a picture frame.

Test Preparation

✔ **Write** the letter of the correct answer.

1. Last month Ali ___ some tomatoes.

  ○ **A** plants
  ○ **B** planted
  ○ **C** will plan

2. Now he ___ the plants.

  ○ **A** plants
  ○ **B** planted
  ○ **C** will plant

3. Tomorrow he ___ weeds.

  ○ **A** pulls
  ○ **B** pulled
  ○ **C** will pull

4. Last winter Ali ___ of fresh tomatoes.

  ○ **A** dreams
  ○ **B** dreamed
  ○ **C** will dream

5. Next week he ___ big red tomatoes.

  ○ **A** picks
  ○ **B** picked
  ○ **C** will pick

6. Now Ali ___ in the yard.

  ○ **A** waits
  ○ **B** waited
  ○ **C** will wait

Review

☑ **Choose** the correct verb in ( ).
Write the sentences.

1. The baby (crawls, crawled) now.

2. Soon she (walked, will walk).

3. Last month she (rolls, rolled) over.

4. In the future, she (talked, will talk).

5. Now she (makes, will make) silly sounds.

6. Yesterday she (laughs, laughed).

☑ **Add** -s, -ed, or will to each verb in ( ).
Write the sentences.

7. Yesterday Manuel (walk) to the park.

8. Now he (feed) his baby sister.

9. Now she (bang) her spoon on the table.

10. In an hour, Manuel (clean) the kitchen.

11. Last week he (visit) his aunt.

12. Later tonight, he (call) Jeff on the phone.

Vivid Words

Use **vivid words**. Help your readers see, hear, taste, smell, and touch what you are describing.

Not Vivid I <u>looked</u> at the <u>flowers</u>.

Vivid I <u>gazed</u> at the <u>bright yellow pansies</u>.

 Replace the underlined word in each sentence with a more vivid word from the box. **Write** the new sentences.

drifted	perfect	thrilled	tore

1. I found a <u>nice</u> gift for my mother.

2. She <u>took</u> off the wrapping paper.

3. The paper <u>fell</u> to the ground.

4. She was <u>happy</u> with the teacup.

 Describe something in your classroom. **Use** vivid words to show readers how it looks, sounds, tastes, smells, or feels.

Write an Ad

Writing Prompt Imagine that you have created a new food. Decide what the food looks and tastes like. Give it a name. Then write an ad for the food. Use your ideas to make people want to buy your food.

Writer mentions new food in title.

Questions get reader interested right away.

Vivid words help reader "see" the food.

Try New Broc Puffs!

Are you tired of potato chips and pretzels? Do you think all snack foods are bad for you? Try new Broc Puffs. Broc Puffs are crispy, puffy little pillows. They taste just like fresh broccoli and creamy cheese. Eat as many as you want! This snack food is good for you. Broc Puffs are full of vitamins. Yummy <u>and</u> healthful—that's new Broc Puffs!

Am, Is, Are, Was, and Were

The verbs **am, is, are, was,** and **were** do not show action. They show what someone or something is or was. These verbs are forms of the verb **to be.**

The verbs **am, is,** and **are** tell about now.

I **am** an inventor.   Jen **is** an inventor.
Des and Ali **are** inventors.

The verbs **was** and **were** tell about the past.

Bill **was** an inventor.
Kate and Sean **were** inventors.

Use **am, is,** and **was** to tell about one person, place, or thing. Use **are** and **were** to tell about more than one person, place, or thing.

A **Write** each sentence. **Underline** the verb.

1. George Washington Carver is one of my heroes.

2. He was a great man.

3. Plants were important to him.

4. I am in the library.

5. These books are about Carver's work.

B **Write** the verb in ( ) that completes each sentence.

1. Inventors ___ clever people. (is, are)

2. Zippers ___ a great invention. (was, were)

3. Today inventions ___ everywhere. (is, are)

4. I ___ in the Young Inventors Club. (am, are)

5. George ___ in the club too. (are, is)

C **Write** the sentences. **Use** a verb from the box.
Write N if the verb tells about now. **Write** P
if the verb tells about the past.

am	is	are
was	were	

6. I ___ seven years old now.

7. My brother ___ nine.

8. Yesterday we ___ inventors.

9. Our invention ___ a robot.

10. Today we ___ explorers.

Test Preparation

✓ **Write** the letter of the correct answer.

1. A sweet potato ___ a vegetable.
- ○ **A** is
- ○ **B** are
- ○ **C** were

2. Vegetables ___ good for you.
- ○ **A** am
- ○ **B** are
- ○ **C** was

3. Tomatoes and beans ___ in my garden.
- ○ **A** was
- ○ **B** is
- ○ **C** were

4. One tomato ___ very big.
- ○ **A** are
- ○ **B** am
- ○ **C** was

5. I ___ in the kitchen now.
- ○ **A** is
- ○ **B** am
- ○ **C** was

6. The sweet potatoes ___ in a pie.
- ○ **A** are
- ○ **B** is
- ○ **C** was

Review

✓ **Write** each sentence. **Underline** the verb.
Write *N* if the verb tells about now. **Write** *P*
if the verb tells about the past.

   1. I am hungry.

   2. Dad is in the kitchen.

   3. The sandwiches were on a plate.

   4. My sandwich was peanut butter.

   5. Dad and I are full now.

✓ **Choose** the verb in ( ) that completes each
sentence. **Write** the sentences.

   6. Uncle George (is, am) a painter.

   7. Once he (was, is) a farmer.

   8. I (am, is) at his farm.

   9. First we (was, were) in the house.

   10. Now we (were, are) in the barn.

   11. His paintings (is, are) on the walls.

   12. One picture (is, are) of a cow.

Use Precise Words

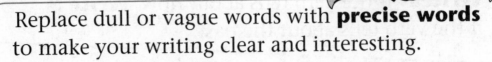

Replace dull or vague words with **precise words** to make your writing clear and interesting.

No   Mr. Kim is nice.
Yes   Mr. Kim always smiles and says hello.

 Which sentence in each pair uses precise words?
Write the sentence.

1. Jose got a lot of stuff for his birthday.
Jose got video games and a basketball
for his birthday.

2. We saw lions and elephants at the zoo.
We saw animals at the zoo.

3. I had a good time at camp.
I paddled a canoe at camp.

4. Cara pushed her books into her backpack.
Cara put her things in her bag.

 Write about something you use every day, such
as a toothbrush or a pen. **Use** precise words.

Tell About an Invention

Writing Prompt Tell about an important invention. Explain what it does and why you think it is important. Tell how the invention has changed people's lives.

The Invention of Airplanes

Writer states opinion in opening sentence.

Details support opinion.

Writer compares life before and after airplanes.

I think airplanes are an important invention. Airplanes let people travel a long way in a short time. Before there were airplanes, people had to travel by horse, wagon, train, or ship. These trips took a long time. Horses, wagons, trains, and ships could not go everywhere in the world. With airplanes, people can go almost anywhere they want. Also, they can get there quickly.

Adjectives and Our Senses

An **adjective** describes a person, place, animal, or thing. An **adjective** can tell how something looks, sounds, tastes, feels, or smells.

My family loves **hot** cornbread.

Hot describes the way the cornbread tastes and feels.

A **Write** the adjective in each sentence that tells how something looks, sounds, tastes, feels, or smells.

1. Grandmother baked with yellow cornmeal.

2. She put in flour, eggs, and cold milk.

3. Grandmother added pepper and green chilies.

4. She stirred everything into a smooth batter.

5. She poured the batter into shiny pans.

6. Now I make delicious cornbread too.

B **Find** the sentence with the adjective. **Write** the sentence. **Underline** the adjective.

1. We buy colorful cloth.
   Gina and I choose it.

2. Gina and I begin.
   We sew warm quilts.

3. I use red squares.
   I make squares and circles.

4. Gina likes stars and triangles.
   Gina cuts big stars.

5. We sew with needles and thread.
   We hum quiet tunes.

C **Complete** each sentence with an adjective of your own. **Tell** how something looks, sounds, tastes, feels, or smells. **Write** the sentences.

6. Dad makes ___ chicken.

7. I mix ___ lemonade.

8. Mom drives down ___ roads.

9. We smell ___ grass.

10. Birds sing ___ songs.

Test Preparation

✓ **Write** the letter of the correct answer.

1. Raccoons have ___ tails.
- ○ **A** wash
- ○ **B** paw
- ○ **C** long

2. Squirrels have ___ teeth.
- ○ **A** nut
- ○ **B** tree
- ○ **C** sharp

3. Mice have ___ fur.
- ○ **A** ear
- ○ **B** soft
- ○ **C** sharp

4. Crows make ___ caws.
- ○ **A** loud
- ○ **B** fly
- ○ **C** was

5. Skunks spray ___ smells.
- ○ **A** bad
- ○ **B** fur
- ○ **C** run

6. Bees make ___ honey.
- ○ **A** sting
- ○ **B** sweet
- ○ **C** buzz

Review

✓ **Choose** the word in ( ) that completes each sentence. **Write** the sentences.

1. This is my (was, warm) jacket.

2. I wrap (thick, put) quilts around me.

3. I drink a mug of (find, hot) chocolate.

4. I put on (fuzzy, wear) socks.

5. (Are, Soft) mittens keep my hands warm.

6. (Wrap, Fresh) bread smells wonderful.

✓ **Write** each sentence. **Underline** the adjective.

7. People like quiet bedrooms.

8. Jenny's room has gray walls.

9. Shiny stars glow above her.

10. Smooth floors creak and groan.

11. Windows let in cold air.

12. Branches tap on frosty glass.

Use Strong Adjectives

Strong adjectives make vivid word pictures for your readers.

Weak Adjective   Sue wore a <u>nice</u> hat.

Strong Adjective   Sue wore a <u>floppy</u> hat.

 Look at the underlined adjectives. Which sentence in each pair has a stronger adjective? **Write** the sentence.

1. Aunt June sent me a <u>pretty</u> scarf.
Aunt June sent me a <u>red-and-gold</u> scarf.

2. They served <u>fruity</u> punch at the party.
They served <u>good</u> punch at the party.

3. The plane was late because of <u>bad</u> weather.
The plane was late because of <u>stormy</u> weather.

4. He grows <u>fine</u> tomatoes in his garden.
He grows <u>juicy</u> tomatoes in his garden.

 Describe your favorite place. **Use** strong adjectives to make a vivid picture of the place.

Write a Riddle

Writing Prompt Choose two things that can be compared, such as two seasons. Write two riddles. Give clues that describe the two things.

What Is It?

Riddles describe the seasons but do not name them.

It has warm days but cool nights. Rain falls in steady showers. Snow melts away. Colorful tulips bloom, and the brown grass becomes green.

Answer: Spring

Strong adjectives help readers picture each season.

Short and long sentences add variety to writing.

Its days and nights are cool. The leaves on the trees turn red, orange, and gold. Then they fall to the ground. A strong wind blows the dry leaves into small piles.

Answer: Fall

Adjectives for Number, Size, and Shape

> Words for number, size, and shape are
> **adjectives**.
>
> The words **a** and **an** are also adjectives.
>
> **A round** pumpkin has **large** seeds.
>
> The word **a** describes how many
> pumpkins—one.
>
> **Round** describes the shape of the pumpkin.
> **Large** describes the size of the seeds.

A **Write** the adjective in each sentence. Then **write**
number, size, or *shape* to tell what it describes.

1. Tina planted ten sunflowers.
2. Sunflowers are tall plants.
3. They have big stalks.
4. Seeds grow in large heads.
5. Tina took out oval seeds.
6. She filled five bags with seeds.
7. Tina's garden has twenty tulips.
8. Tulips grow from round bulbs.

B **Find** the adjective that completes each sentence. **Use** the clue in ( ) for help. **Write** the sentences.

1. My class visited ___ pumpkin patch. (number)
   long   a   huge

2. There were ___ stacks of pumpkins. (size)
   square   colorful   tall

3. Each child chose ___ pumpkin. (number)
   one   oval   thin

4. Maria and Kevin picked ___ pumpkins. (shape)
   seven   orange   round

5. I liked ___ pumpkins best. (size)
   one   little   new

C **Choose** an adjective of your own to complete each sentence. **Use** the clue in ( ). **Write** the sentences.

6. Here are ___ pies. (shape)

7. You can cut a pie into ___ pieces. (number)

8. I like ___ pieces. (size)

9. You need ___ cherries for pie. (size)

10. Use ___ pumpkin for each pie. (number)

Test Preparation

☑ **Write** the letter of the correct answer.

1. This apple had ___ seeds.
   - ○ **A** run
   - ○ **B** six
   - ○ **C** go

2. Do ___ apples have more seeds?
   - ○ **A** large
   - ○ **B** chew
   - ○ **C** fill

3. Those ___ seeds come from sunflowers.
   - ○ **A** fast
   - ○ **B** oval
   - ○ **C** plant

4. The ___ peas on your plate are seeds.
   - ○ **A** round
   - ○ **B** cook
   - ○ **C** swim

5. Pieces of corn from ___ cob are seeds.
   - ○ **A** cut
   - ○ **B** farmer
   - ○ **C** a

6. You might eat ___ seeds on bread.
   - ○ **A** grow
   - ○ **B** stick
   - ○ **C** tiny

Review

☑ **Choose** the adjective in ( ) that completes each sentence. **Write** the sentences.

    1. Here is (an, vine) orange pumpkin.

    2. Make a (stir, giant) pot of pumpkin soup.

    3. Put the soup into (round, pour) bowls.

    4. Eat the soup with (square, spoon) crackers.

    5. Roast (pan, eighty) pumpkin seeds.

    6. Store the seeds in (wrap, small) bags.

☑ **Write** the sentences. **Underline** the adjective in each sentence.

    7. Squashes grow on long vines.

    8. Oval watermelons grow on vines.

    9. Thin vines may climb poles.

    10. Vines can crawl up a fence.

    11. Two vines can twist together.

    12. Oranges and lemons grow on short trees.

Show, Don't Tell

When you write about something, **show—don't tell**—how it looks, sounds, tastes, smells, or feels.

No   I ate a peach.

Yes   I bit into a ripe peach, and juice ran down my chin.

 Choose words from the box to replace the underlined words in each sentence. **Write** the new sentences.

crackles across the sky

crying and shaking

shouted and clapped

1. He was <u>scared</u>.

2. Lightning <u>is loud</u>.

3. The children <u>made noise</u>.

 What is the weather like today? **Describe** it. **Show, don't tell,** how it looks, sounds, and feels.

Write a Food Review

> **Writing Prompt**   Write a review of a food that a relative makes. Describe the food and tell whether you like it or not and why.

Writer states opinion of the pie.

Strong adjectives make a vivid picture of the pie.

Writer shows rather than tells reader about the pie.

Aunt Sue's Pumpkin Pie

Aunt Sue's pumpkin pie is the best! It has a thin, flaky crust. The filling is creamy and smooth. The filling melts in your mouth. Aunt Sue uses cinnamon, ginger, and cloves in the filling. How do I know she has just made pumpkin pie? I can smell the spices in her house! I love this pie.

Adjectives That Compare

Add **-er** to an adjective to compare two persons, places, or things.

Add **-est** to an adjective to compare three or more persons, places, or things.

The chick is **smaller** than the hen.

Smaller compares two things—the chick and the hen.

The egg is **smallest** of the three.

Smallest compares three things—the egg, the chick, and the hen.

A **Write** the sentences. **Circle** adjectives that compare two things. **Underline** adjectives that compare three or more things.

    1. Lions are faster than zebras.

    2. The cheetah is the fastest animal on land.

    3. The blue whale is the longest animal of all.

    4. Dolphins are longer than porpoises.

B **Choose** the adjective in ( ) that completes each sentence. **Write** the sentences.

1. A lamb is (shorter, shortest) than a calf.

2. A chick is (shorter, shortest) of all.

3. A kitten is (taller, tallest) than a mouse.

4. A cat is (taller, tallest) of the three.

5. A turtle is (slower, slowest) of all.

6. A cow is (slower, slowest) than a rabbit.

C **Add** *-er* or *-est* to the word in ( ) to complete each sentence. **Write** the sentences.

7. This pond is ___ of all the forest ponds. (deep)

8. It is ___ now than last night. (quiet)

9. The water is ___ in summer than in winter. (warm)

10. That frog is ___ than this fish. (small)

11. The turtle has the ___ shell I have ever seen. (round)

12. Today is the ___ day of the whole week. (cool)

Test Preparation

✓ **Write** the letter of the correct answer.

1. Mary's frog is ___ than Todd's snake.

- ○ **A** green
- ○ **B** greener
- ○ **C** greenest

2. Dan's parrot is the ___ animal of all.

- ○ **A** bright
- ○ **B** brighter
- ○ **C** brightest

3. Mark's shirt is ___ than Lucia's shirt.

- ○ **A** light
- ○ **B** lighter
- ○ **C** lightest

4. Ling's shirt is ___ of the three.

- ○ **A** dark
- ○ **B** darker
- ○ **C** darkest

5. Sara is the ___ child of all.

- ○ **A** old
- ○ **B** older
- ○ **C** oldest

6. Marty is ___ than Jason.

- ○ **A** young
- ○ **B** younger
- ○ **C** youngest

Review

- ✓ **Write** the sentences. **Circle** adjectives that compare two things. **Underline** adjectives that compare three or more things.

    1. Our classroom is colder than yours.

    2. Mei Ling is the tallest girl in the class.

    3. Juan talks louder than Donna.

    4. Luis is smarter than I am.

    5. Who is kindest of all the children?

- ✓ **Add** *-er* or *-est* to the word in ( ) to complete each sentence. **Write** the sentences.

    6. A frog has (few) legs than a crab.

    7. The tadpole is the (small) animal in the pond.

    8. This pond is (clean) of all.

    9. The grass is (green) here than there.

    10. The mud is (soft) than the grass.

Repetition and Rhyme

Sometimes a writer repeats a word or a group of words. This is called **repetition**. Sometimes a writer uses words whose ending sounds are the same. This is called **rhyme**.

Once there was a frog, frog, frog,

Who sat upon a log, log, log.

Repetition *frog* 3 times, *log* 3 times

Rhyme fr*og* and l*og*

 Write the repeated word or words.

1. Cock-a-doodle-do, how are you?

Cock-a-doodle-do, I'll let you know soon.

2. The boys were playing ball. The boys were riding bikes. The boys were having fun!

 Write the words that rhyme.

3. Pat saw a cat. The cat saw a rat. The rat saw a bat. The bat saw Pat.

Write a Song

Writing Prompt Write a song about things you could do when you were a baby or things you can do now. Use a familiar tune, such as "Old MacDonald Had a Farm." Use rhyme.

When I Was Very Small

(to the tune of "Old MacDonald Had a Farm")

I had no teeth, I couldn't talk,

When I was very small.

I had no hair, I couldn't walk,

When I was very small.

I had to crawl from here to there,

I waved my fat arms in the air—oooh,

I ate my mushy vegetables,

When I was very small.

Song has repetition.

Song has rhyme.

Song has several funny lines.

Adverbs That Tell When and Where

Adverbs tell more about a verb. Some adverbs show **when** or **where**.

Today our family is moving.
Today tells when.
I hurry **downstairs.**
Downstairs tells where.

A **Write** the adverb from each sentence. **Write** *when* if the adverb shows when. **Write** *where* if the adverb shows where.

1. I packed my books yesterday.

2. Now I pack my toys.

3. My bike must be somewhere.

4. The movers set the boxes down.

5. The moving van is parked outside.

6. Soon we will get to our new house.

7. We should arrive tomorrow.

8. I will be happy there.

B **Find** the adverb to complete each sentence. **Use** the clue in ( ) to help you. **Write** the sentences.

1. ___ I must find my kitten. (when)

   Call   Now   Spotted

2. Her basket is ___. (where)

   one   see   inside

3. She isn't ___. (where)

   here   can   tell

4. I search ___ for my kitten. (where)

   jump   many   everywhere

5. ___ I find her asleep in a box. (when)

   Fun   Play   Then

C **Choose** an adverb from the box to complete each sentence. **Use** the clue in ( ). **Write** the sentences.

outside   always   now   today   somewhere

6. I (when) lose things.

7. (When) I lost my rocks.

8. They were (where) in the backyard.

9. I will start looking for them (when).

10. My rocks must be (where).

Test Preparation

✓ **Write** the letter of the correct answer.

1. Two kittens are ___.
- ○ **A** for
- ○ **B** inside
- ○ **C** purr

2. I will choose a kitten ___.
- ○ **A** paws
- ○ **B** see
- ○ **C** today

3. A gray kitten ran ___.
- ○ **A** here
- ○ **B** fur
- ○ **C** pretty

4. I reached ___.
- ○ **A** down
- ○ **B** few
- ○ **C** want

5. ___ I touched its soft fur.
- ○ **A** Far
- ○ **B** Then
- ○ **C** Go

6. ___ the kitten is mine.
- ○ **A** Round
- ○ **B** Like
- ○ **C** Now

Review

✓ **Choose** the adverb in ( ) that completes each sentence. **Write** the sentences.

1. Trucks carry things (everywhere, beside).

2. (Around, Yesterday) this truck hauled cars.

3. Vans move people (far, never).

4. This tank truck (near, always) carries milk.

5. (Upstairs, Tomorrow) that truck will haul steel.

✓ **Write** the adverb from each sentence. **Write** *when* if the adverb shows when. **Write** *where* if the adverb shows where.

6. Greg went to a new school today.

7. He walked inside.

8. There everyone welcomed him.

9. Greg walked upstairs to his classroom.

10. His locker was nearby.

Sound Words

> **Sound words** are words that sound like the sounds they name.
>
>   Bees <u>buzz</u> by me.
>
> Say the word *buzz*. It sounds like the sound that bees make.

 Write the sound word in each sentence.

1. The soda fizzes in the glass.

2. She shut the screen door with a bang.

3. A snake hissed in the grass.

4. He slurped soup from a mug.

5. The lion's roar scared the small child.

6. The chick cheeps for its mother.

7. The happy kitten purrs.

8. We heard the ding-dong of the school bell.

 Imagine you are standing by a busy street. **Describe** what you hear and see. **Use** as many sound words as you can.

Write a Poem

Writing Prompt   Write a poem about moving. Tell how you feel about moving to a new place, home, or school.

Writer uses rhyme to make poem fun to read.

Writer shows feelings and how they change.

Writer uses repetition to make poem lively.

Writer uses sound words to make a vivid picture.

We are in our new house.
I don't like it at all.
My door doesn't creak,
My floor doesn't squeak,
And the bathroom is way down the hall.

Shh! Wait! Did you hear that?
It's not so bad, after all.
My floor just creaked,
My door just squeaked,
And I can slide—whoosh—down the hall!

Adverbs That Tell How

An **adverb** can tell more about a verb by telling **how** an action is done. Adverbs that tell how usually end in **-ly**.

When Dad looked up, he saw the dark clouds **clearly.**

Clearly tells *how* Dad saw the clouds.

A **Write** each sentence. **Underline** the adverb that tells how.

1. We listened carefully to Dad's words.

2. We quickly went to a safe place.

3. We sat quietly in the basement.

4. The wind blew wildly.

5. Thunder boomed loudly.

6. We heard all the noises clearly.

7. Suddenly the basement was dark.

8. We waited silently for the lights.

B **Write** the sentence. **Use** the word in ( ) that tells how.

1. The storm ends (quickly, rain).

2. The sun shines (brightly, breeze).

3. Birds (flying, sweetly) sing.

4. The wind blows (always, softly).

5. The streets dry (far, slowly).

6. (Carefully, Late) I open the door.

C **Write** each sentence with an adverb that tells how. **Use** each adverb once.

7. My sister sings ___.

8. The baby cries ___.

9. The man speaks ___.

| loudly |
| slowly |
| softly |

10. Her brother walks ___.

11. That woman dances ___.

12. He climbs ___.

| carefully |
| quickly |
| badly |

Test Preparation

✓ **Write** the letter of the correct answer.

1. I fell ___.

   ○ **A** tomorrow
   ○ **B** suddenly
   ○ **C** trip

2. I called ___ for help.

   ○ **A** loudly
   ○ **B** close
   ○ **C** phone

3. ___ Dad rushed in.

   ○ **A** Around
   ○ **B** Hurry
   ○ **C** Quickly

4. He checked me ___.

   ○ **A** never
   ○ **B** looked
   ○ **C** carefully

5. Dad held ice ___ on my foot.

   ○ **A** tightly
   ○ **B** ahead
   ○ **C** cube

6. ___ I felt better.

   ○ **A** Cold
   ○ **B** Slowly
   ○ **C** Up

Review

☑ **Write** the sentence that has an adverb.

1. Ms. Ling is a good teacher.
   Helen learned quickly.

2. Ms. Ling carefully wrote letters.
   Helen printed them.

3. Ms. Ling read a story.
   Helen gladly told about it.

4. The teacher smiled proudly at Helen.
   Helen thanked her.

☑ **Choose** the adverb that completes each sentence.
Write the sentences.

5. Snow fell ___ all day.
   lightly   kindly   warmly

6. I walked ___ into the snow.
   badly   neatly   bravely

7. ___ a rabbit hopped past.
   Suddenly   Brightly   Slowly

8. I ___ slipped on some ice.
   freshly   nearly   deeply

Focus/Ideas

> A good paragraph has a main idea. The **main idea** is what the paragraph is about. Each sentence in the paragraph should tell about the main idea. When you are writing a paragraph, make every sentence **focus** on your main idea.

Which two sentences in each paragraph do NOT focus on the main idea? **Write** the sentences.

1. Every summer I go to the beach with my family. Mountains are nice too. I dig in the sand and splash in the water. Where are my hiking shoes? The beach is my favorite place.

2. Two months ago Travis planted tomato seeds. Last year he planted pumpkin seeds. The tiny tomato seeds grew into large green plants. Soon Travis will pick ripe tomatoes. Tomatoes and carrots are good in salads.

Write a paragraph about your favorite season. **Make sure** every sentence focuses on the main idea of the paragraph.

Describe the Weather

Writing Prompt Choose a kind of storm. Imagine the storm is happening right now. Write a paragraph about what the storm looks, sounds, and feels like.

Main idea comes in the first sentence.

Vivid words give a clear picture of the hurricane.

All sentences focus on telling about the hurricane.

Weather News

We are in the middle of a hurricane. A hurricane brings heavy rain and strong winds. Rain is pouring down. The wind is blowing very hard. You can't stand or walk outside. Water fills the streets and yards. Before the storm, my dad and I covered the windows. My mom carried food, water, and candles to the second floor. We moved upstairs because we are safer there.

Pronouns

A **pronoun** is a word that takes the place of a noun or nouns. The words **he, she, it, we, you,** and **they** are pronouns.

Rosa is a doctor. **She** helps people.

She takes the place of the noun **Rosa.**

Dan and **Marie** are nurses. **They** help people.

They replaces the nouns **Dan** and **Marie.**

A **Write** the pronoun that can take the place of the underlined word or words.

1. <u>Animals</u> come to Dr. Soto.
   They   We   You

2. <u>Alice Johnson</u> helps run the town.
   It   She   He

3. <u>Jason and I</u> pick up trash.
   You   We   She

4. <u>Mr. Jones</u> takes food to sick people.
   She   He   It

5. <u>The fire truck</u> is shiny and new.
   He   We   It

B **Write** the pronoun that can take the place of the underlined word or words. **Use** *he, she, it, we,* or *they.*

1. <u>Sue Krensky</u> talks to the children at school.

2. <u>The children</u> listen to the police officer.

3. <u>Juan and I</u> want to be police officers.

4. <u>Juan</u> asks Officer Krensky many questions.

5. Someday <u>the dream</u> will come true.

C **Read** the pairs of sentences. **Choose** a pronoun to fill in each blank. **Use** *he, she, it, we,* or *they.* **Write** the new sentences.

6. Uncle Ralph is a firefighter.
   ___ knows about fires.

7. This helmet belongs to Uncle Ralph.
   ___ protects his head.

8. Hoses are on the fire truck.
   ___ spray water on the fire.

9. Beth Mills drives the fire truck.
   ___ has to drive fast.

10. My sister and I go to the fire station.
    ___ visit Uncle Ralph.

Test Preparation

✓ **Mark** the letter of the correct pronoun.

1. <u>Nancy Loo</u> is a weather reporter.
   - ○ **A** We
   - ○ **B** She
   - ○ **C** It

2. <u>The weather</u> is important to many people.
   - ○ **A** It
   - ○ **B** They
   - ○ **C** We

3. <u>The children</u> invited Ms. Loo to their class.
   - ○ **A** You
   - ○ **B** They
   - ○ **C** He

4. <u>Brian</u> asked a question about hail.
   - ○ **A** We
   - ○ **B** It
   - ○ **C** He

5. <u>Consuelo and I</u> asked about sleet.
   - ○ **A** You
   - ○ **B** He
   - ○ **C** We

6. <u>Ms. Loo</u> told us about cold fronts.
   - ○ **A** She
   - ○ **B** We
   - ○ **C** They

Review

✓ **Write** each sentence. **Underline** the pronoun.

1. Will you get a job someday?
2. She will work on computers.
3. We will fix cars.
4. They want to work with animals.
5. Maybe he will be a vet.
6. It is a useful job.

✓ **Rewrite** each sentence. **Change** the underlined word or words to *he, she, it, we,* or *they.*

7. The fire station is busy today.
8. Lisa checks the siren.
9. Dan and Dave wash the fire truck.
10. Mario cooks in the kitchen.
11. Maya and I test the air tanks.
12. The air tanks must be full.

Word Choice

Choose words carefully. Use exact nouns, strong verbs, and exciting adjectives. They will make your writing clear and lively.

No He <u>had</u> a <u>nice</u> sweater.

Yes <u>Jack</u> <u>wore</u> a <u>blue and red striped</u> sweater.

Write the sentence in each pair that sounds more interesting.

1. A person was here.
A firefighter visited our class.

2. She showed us stuff.
Ms. Li showed us her helmet and boots.

3. We learned rules for fire safety.
We learned new things.

4. The firefighter told some stories.
The firefighter told exciting stories about rescues.

Write about a job you would like to have.
Choose your words carefully.

Give an Award

> **Writing Prompt** Give an award to a community worker, such as a firefighter, police officer, teacher, or librarian. Tell what the person does. Explain why he or she deserves the award.

Person chosen for the award is introduced in the first sentence.

Writer gives reasons to support her choice.

Careful word choice gives readers a clear picture of the person.

And the Award Goes to . . .

I think we should give an award to Mr. Grant. He is the best teacher I have ever had. He makes learning exciting and interesting. That is important. He wants us to ask questions. Sometimes he answers them, but mostly he helps us find the answers for ourselves. He is always patient, even when we don't understand something the first time. He just explains it another way.

Pronouns for One and More Than One

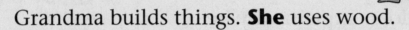

He, she, and **it** are pronouns that name only one.

We and **they** are pronouns that name more than one.

Grandma builds things. **She** uses wood.

She is a pronoun that names one person—Grandma.

Grandma and I worked. **We** built a birdhouse.

We is a pronoun that names more than one—Grandma and I.

A **Write** the sentences. **Circle** the pronouns that name only one. **Underline** the pronouns that name more than one.

1. On the way home one night, we saw a cat.

2. It was sitting by the side of the road.

3. Mom said we should stop.

4. She handed Dad a blanket.

5. He wrapped the blanket around the cat.

6. They took the cat to a vet.

B **Write** the pronoun in ( ) that can take the place of the underlined word or words.

1. <u>Travis and I</u> visit Grandma and Grandpa. (We, He)

2. <u>Grandma</u> wants a planter box. (They, She)

3. <u>Grandma and I</u> nail boards together. (We, She)

4. <u>Grandpa</u> has a truck. (They, He)

5. <u>The truck</u> is bright red. (They, It)

6. <u>Grandpa and Travis</u> drive to the store. (They, He)

C **Write** a new sentence about the underlined word or words in each sentence. **Use** *he, she, it, we,* or *they* in your sentence.

Example   <u>My sisters and I</u> got a kitten.
                    We were very excited.

7. <u>Kittens</u> are baby cats.

8. <u>Sara</u> wants a name for the kitten.

9. <u>Martha and I</u> have another name.

10. <u>Dad</u> doesn't like our names.

Test Preparation

✓ **Mark** the letter of the pronoun that can take the place of the underlined word or words.

1. <u>Storms</u> can be loud.
   - ○ **A** She
   - ○ **B** We
   - ○ **C** They

2. <u>A high wind</u> can blow down trees.
   - ○ **A** They
   - ○ **B** It
   - ○ **C** He

3. <u>Patty and I</u> do not like thunder.
   - ○ **A** He
   - ○ **B** It
   - ○ **C** We

4. <u>Dad</u> says lightning can hurt people.
   - ○ **A** He
   - ○ **B** They
   - ○ **C** We

5. <u>Ice storms</u> make roads slick.
   - ○ **A** They
   - ○ **B** He
   - ○ **C** She

6. <u>Mom</u> loves snow.
   - ○ **A** We
   - ○ **B** She
   - ○ **C** They

Review

✔ **Write** the pronoun in each sentence. **Write** *one* if the pronoun names only one. **Write** *more than one* if the pronoun names more than one.

1. The kitten was outside, and Kevin found it.

2. Where did he look?

3. We will ask Sara.

4. She says Kevin looked in the yard.

5. Will they keep the kitten?

✔ **Write** each sentence. **Replace** the underlined word or words. **Use** *he, she, it, we,* or *they.*

6. <u>Animals</u> come in many colors.

7. <u>Calvin</u> has a green lizard.

8. <u>Louisa</u> bought an orange fish.

9. <u>Paul</u> got a blue and red bird.

10. <u>Beth and I</u> found a brown puppy.

Use Persuasive Words

A writer wants readers to agree with his or her opinion. The writer **uses words** such as *should, need, must, best, worst,* and *most important* **to persuade readers.**

Use the words from the box to complete the letter. **Write** the letter.

Word Bank
important
best
need
should

Dear Mom,

    I think we **(1)** ___ visit Washington, D.C., this summer. We can see the White House and many other famous buildings. All Americans **(2)** ___ to learn about their nation's capital. Visiting Washington would be the **(3)** ___ trip we could take. Most **(4)** ___, we could do it together!

                      Love,
                      Zoe

Write a letter to a parent telling about a trip you would like to take. **Give** reasons for the trip. **Use** words that persuade.

Write Reasons

Writing Prompt Explain why you should have a pet. Tell the kind of pet you want, and give reasons to support your idea.

Words are used to persuade readers that this is a good idea.

Writer gives reasons to support idea.

Writer saves most important reason for last.

Why We Should Have a Pet

I think we should get a dog. Tad and I study hard and get good grades. We always do our chores. A dog would be the best reward that we could get. Also, we are responsible. We will take care of a dog. Most important, a dog could protect our house when we are away.

Using *I* and *Me*

The pronouns **I** and **me** take the place of your name. Use **I** in the subject of a sentence. Use **me** after an action verb. Always write **I** with a capital letter.

I always wanted a dog. Mom bought **me** one.

When you talk about yourself and another person or thing, name yourself last. The pronouns **I** and **me** take the place of your name.

The dog and **I** sing together.
People give the dog and **me** special awards.

Ⓐ Use *I* or *me* to complete each sentence. **Write** the sentences.

1. ___ have a dog named Pepper.

2. Pepper and ___ are best friends.

3. Dad teaches Pepper and ___ funny songs.

4. Singing makes Pepper and ___ happy.

5. Maybe Pepper and ___ can sing for you.

6. Invite Pepper and ___ to your house.

B **Find** the word or words that complete each sentence. **Write** the sentences.

1. ___ are good pet owners.
Ali and I   Ali and me   me and Ali

2. ___ keep Bingo on a leash in the park.
me   I   i

3. Bingo walks next to ___.
me and Ali   Ali and I   Ali and me

4. Ali helps ___ with Bingo's bath.
I   i   me

C **Answer** each question. **Add** words to finish each sentence. **Use** *I* or *me* in the sentences.

5. Did you go to the pet store?
Yes, ___.

6. Who went with you?
James ___.

7. What kind of bird did you see?
He and ___.

8. What did the bird do?
The bird ___ James and ___.

Test Preparation

✓ **Mark** the letter of the correct answer.

1. ___ like baseball.
   - ○ **A** I
   - ○ **B** i
   - ○ **C** me

2. ___ go to a baseball game.
   - ○ **A** I and Mom
   - ○ **B** Mom and I
   - ○ **C** Mom and me

3. Mom buys ___ popcorn.
   - ○ **A** I
   - ○ **B** me
   - ○ **C** he

4. A ball almost hits ___.
   - ○ **A** Mom and I
   - ○ **B** me and Mom
   - ○ **C** Mom and me

5. ___ jump for the ball.
   - ○ **A** i
   - ○ **B** me
   - ○ **C** I

6. The ball just misses ___.
   - ○ **A** me
   - ○ **B** I
   - ○ **C** Mom and I

Review

✔ **Choose** the word in ( ) that completes each sentence. **Write** the sentences.

1. (I, Me) have a dog that does tricks.

2. Sparky can bring (I, me) balls.

3. Jerry and (I, me) hide from Sparky.

4. Sparky finds Jerry and (I, me).

5. Let (I, me) show you his new trick.

✔ **Write** the sentence that uses *I* or *me* correctly. **Underline** *I* or *me*.

6. Rosa and me care for our class hamster.
Rosa and I feed the hamster.

7. I bring it fresh water.
The hamster shows Rosa and I its tricks.

8. Me and Rosa clean out its cage.
Rosa and I do not like that job.

9. Mr. Davis helps Rosa and I.
He hands me the hamster.

10. Rosa and me took good care of the pet.
The class thanked Rosa and me.

Know Your Audience

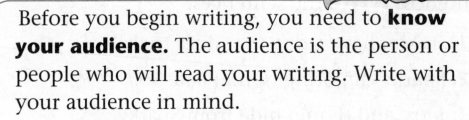

Before you begin writing, you need to **know your audience.** The audience is the person or people who will read your writing. Write with your audience in mind.

To a Friend   Sorry about the mix-up, Dave!

To a Teacher   I'm sorry I forgot the date of the field trip.

Write the letter of the audience that matches each group of sentences best.

A Your classmates   **B** Your older sister
   C The editor of your local paper

1. Your idea for Mom's gift is OK with me. Let's go to the mall on Saturday.

2. Our town will be 125 years old next year. We need to plan a special celebration.

3. Ms. Huber's birthday is next Thursday. What are we going to give her?

Write a note to an older relative thanking him or her for a gift. **Think** about your audience.

Write Pet Care Rules

Writing Prompt Write your classmates a set of rules for taking care of a pet. Think about your audience.

Writer uses words and voice that are suitable for the audience.

Rules are put in a numbered list to make them easy to read.

Writer gives reasons to help explain some rules.

Pet Care Rules

1. Your pet must be fed every day. Choose the right food.

2. Your pet needs fresh water every day. Keep the dish in the same place.

3. You should spend time with your pet. Animals get lonely too.

4. Don't let your pet roam outside. Pets need to be safe.

5. It is important to take your pet to a vet every year. Animals need a checkup too.

Different Kinds of Pronouns

The pronouns **I, he, she, we,** and **they** are used as subjects of sentences.

The pronouns **me, him, her, us,** and **them** are used after action verbs.

The pronouns **you** and **it** can be used anywhere in a sentence.

Calvin has a new bike. **He** can't ride **it.**

The pronoun **he** is the subject of a sentence.

The pronoun **it** is used after the action verb *ride.*

Calvin is riding the bike. Angela helped **him.**

The pronoun **him** is used after the action verb *helped.*

A **Write** the pronoun in each sentence. **Write** *Subject* or *After action verb* to tell where it is used.

1. Sally helped me ride a bike.

2. It got a flat tire.

3. Dad drove over and found us.

4. He took Sally home.

B **Choose** the pronoun in ( ) that can take the place of the underlined word or words. **Write** the sentences.

1. <u>Friends</u> help each other. (They, Them)

2. Dee gave <u>Morris</u> singing lessons. (he, him)

3. <u>Boris</u> helped Alice skate. (He, Him)

4. Paul read <u>Nancy</u> a story. (she, her)

5. Pablo made <u>Jan and Ray</u> soup. (they, them)

6. How can you help <u>your friends</u>? (we, us)

C **Choose** pronouns from the box to take the place of the underlined words. **Write** the sentences.

it	her	they
we	us	she

7. <u>Jon and I</u> will go exploring.

8. Lisa told <u>Jon and me</u> about a good place.

9. <u>Lisa</u> said we could explore there.

10. We asked <u>Lisa</u> where the place is.

11. Lisa said <u>the place</u> is the library.

12. <u>Our adventures</u> would be in books.

Test Preparation

✓ **Mark** the letter of the correct answer.

1. My friends and ___ wanted some fun.

○ **A** me
○ **B** they
○ **C** I

2. Bess told ___ about finger painting.

○ **A** we
○ **B** us
○ **C** it

3. Bess showed ___ and me some pictures.

○ **A** them
○ **B** they
○ **C** I

4. ___ had painted each one.

○ **A** She
○ **B** Her
○ **C** Him

5. Then ___ all painted pictures.

○ **A** her
○ **B** we
○ **C** it

6. Do ___ like finger painting?

○ **A** me
○ **B** it
○ **C** you

Review

✓ **Write** the pronoun that completes each sentence. **Circle** pronouns used as subjects. **Underline** pronouns used after action verbs.

1. (We, Us) have a new clubhouse.

2. Dad helped (we, us) with the work.

3. All my friends like (he, it).

4. (They, Them) bring games and books.

✓ **Find** the pronoun that takes the place of the underlined word or words. **Write** the sentences.

5. Paco and I like cheese.
   Us   We   Her

6. Mom gave my sister and me two new cheeses.
   we   they   us

7. My sister liked the two cheeses very much.
   them   they   you

8. Paco wanted some cheese too.
   Me   He   Him

Know Your Purpose

> Before you write, you need to **know your purpose.** Your purpose may be to persuade someone, to give information, or to make someone laugh.

 Write the letter of the purpose that matches each topic best.

A Persuade someone
B Give information
C Make someone laugh

1. A joke about a cactus and a porcupine

2. Why we need a bigger playground

3. How cats see in the dark

4. Why people should recycle newspapers

5. A funny story about a pet lizard

6. Facts about beavers

 Write about something funny that happened to you. **Remember** that your purpose is to make your reader laugh.

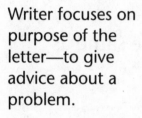

Write a Letter

Writing Prompt   Pretend you are Advice Person. Read the letter from "Puzzled." Write a letter giving advice to "Puzzled."

Dear Advice Person,

   My friend borrows my books and toys. Then he never returns them. What should I do?

                                    Puzzled

Writer focuses on purpose of the letter—to give advice about a problem.

Writing follows the correct letter form.

Writer uses pronouns correctly.

Dear Puzzled,

   Speak up! Ask your friend to return all your books and toys. Maybe he just forgot he had them. Then think twice before you let him borrow anything else. If you do, be sure your name is on everything. Make a list of what you lend him.

   You might invite your friend over to your house to play. Then you can keep your toys and books at home.

                                    Advice Person

Contractions

A **contraction** is a short way to put two words together. An **apostrophe (')** takes the place of one or more letters. Contractions can be formed by putting together a pronoun and another word, such as *will, are,* or *is.*

We will clean up. **We'll** clean up.

Many contractions are formed with verbs and the word *not.*

We **were not** careful. We **weren't** careful.

A **Write** the contraction that means the same as the underlined words.

   1. I <u>did not</u> spill paint on purpose.
       don't   didn't   doesn't

   2. Tina <u>could not</u> get out of the way.
       couldn't   can't   shouldn't

   3. Now <u>she is</u> covered with paint.
       he's   she'll   she's

   4. Dad <u>is not</u> too mad at us.
       weren't   isn't   wasn't

B **Replace** the underlined words with a contraction from the box. **Write** the contraction.

it's	didn't	she's
I'll	don't	we've

1. Tanya's mother said, "<u>Do not</u> go too far."

2. Tanya <u>did not</u> listen to her mother.

3. Now <u>she is</u> lost in the park.

4. <u>We have</u> been looking for her.

5. <u>It is</u> lucky someone found her.

6. Tanya said, "Next time <u>I will</u> listen, Mom."

C **Write** some rules about how to get along with people. **Use** the contractions below in your rules.

7. you'll

8. don't

9. shouldn't

10. you're

11. can't

12. I've

Test Preparation

✓ **Mark** the letter of the correct answer.

1. <u>We are</u> learning about signs.
   - ○ **A** We'll
   - ○ **B** We're
   - ○ **C** They're

2. "<u>Do not</u> walk" is an important sign.
   - ○ **A** Don't
   - ○ **B** Doesn't
   - ○ **C** Didn't

3. <u>I will</u> ask which sign is a triangle.
   - ○ **A** You'll
   - ○ **B** They'll
   - ○ **C** I'll

4. We <u>did not</u> know a stop sign has eight sides.
   - ○ **A** dosn't
   - ○ **B** didn't
   - ○ **C** wouldn't

5. We also learned <u>it is</u> red.
   - ○ **A** she's
   - ○ **B** it'll
   - ○ **C** it's

6. To be safe, we <u>should not</u> forget these signs.
   - ○ **A** shouldn't
   - ○ **B** couldn't
   - ○ **C** wouldn't

Review

✓ **Find** the contraction in ( ) that means the same as the underlined words. **Write** each sentence. **Use** the contraction.

1. Alex <u>has not</u> cleaned his room. (hasn't, isn't)

2. <u>He is</u> busy watching the baby. (He'll, He's)

3. Linda <u>did not</u> make her bed. (didn't, don't)

4. <u>She will</u> make toast for Mom. (She's, She'll)

5. <u>They are</u> good helpers. (They're, They'll)

✓ **Find** each contraction. **Write** the contraction. **Write** the two words that mean the same as the contraction.

6. We'll have a bake sale.

7. The children don't have a sign.

8. We're sure we will need one.

9. One girl couldn't find paint.

10. She's still looking now.

Get Your Reader's Attention

If you want readers to read your writing, you must **get their attention.** Here are two ways:

- Write a title that makes readers curious.
- Write an opening sentence that makes readers want to read on.

Write the title that is more likely to get a reader's attention.

1. My First Day at School
The Day I Was Invisible

Write the opening sentence that is more likely to get a reader's attention.

2. Why would anyone camp in a cow pasture?
We went camping last August.

Write about trying something for the first time. **Write** a title and an opening sentence to get your reader's attention.

Make a Sign

> **Writing Prompt**   Think of something important that you want people to do. Make a sign to persuade them that they should do what you say.

Title grabs reader's attention by asking a question.

Strong opening sentences make reader want to read on.

All sentences focus on purpose of the sign—to persuade.

What Do Your Kids Think?

Do you really know? If you don't, there may be a reason. When was the last time you really talked with your kids? Ask them questions and listen to what they say. How will you know what they are thinking if you don't ask and listen?

Using Capital Letters

Days of the week, months of the year, and **holidays** begin with capital letters.

The first day of **January** is **New Year's Day.**

Titles for people begin with capital letters.

Every year **Mr.** Lewis has a big party.
Coach Landi will order new uniforms.

A **Write** the sentences. **Use** capital letters for the words in ( ).

1. Every (may) our family goes to a baseball game.

2. This is how we spend (memorial day).

3. This holiday is always on a (monday).

4. (dr.) and (mrs.) Carlson bring flags for everyone.

5. Dad packs everything on (sunday).

6. On the (fourth of july), we will go with (officer) Chang to another game.

B **Find** the words that need capital letters. **Write** the words correctly. The number in ( ) tells how many capital letters are needed.

1. st. patrick's day is on march 17. (4)

2. Every year coach Kelly and mrs. O'Malley are in the parade. (2)

3. This year the fourth of july is on a friday. (3)

4. The Bartons and ms. Lutz always go to the barbecue at mr. Garcia's house. (2)

5. Isn't thanksgiving on the fourth thursday in november? (3)

C **Find** the word in the box that completes each sentence. **Write** the sentences. **Use** capital letters.

november	mr.	saturday	miss	flag day

6. ___ James Thomas was a baseball player.

7. He was born on ___ 16, 1941.

8. His favorite holiday is ___.

9. He married ___ Alice Larkin in 1963.

10. The wedding was on a ___.

Test Preparation

✓ **Mark** the letter of the correct answer.

1. My birthday is on ___ 14.
   - ○ **A** january
   - ○ **B** February
   - ○ **C** march

2. I was born on ___.
   - ○ **A** Valentine's day
   - ○ **B** valentine's day
   - ○ **C** Valentine's Day

3. My friend ___ has the same birthday.
   - ○ **A** mrs. Loomis
   - ○ **B** Miss Loomis
   - ○ **C** ms. Loomis

4. This year our birthdays are on ___.
   - ○ **A** Wednesday
   - ○ **B** wednesday
   - ○ **C** wednesDay

5. My sister was born on ___.
   - ○ **A** Labor Day
   - ○ **B** Labor day
   - ○ **C** labor Day

6. Her birthday is in ___.
   - ○ **A** october
   - ○ **B** november
   - ○ **C** September

Review

✓ **Find** the two words that need capital letters in each sentence. **Write** the sentences.

1. Baseball practice runs from april through august.

2. Our coaches are ms. Lopez and dr. Logan.

3. tuesday and thursday are our practice days.

4. The first game is saturday, may 10.

✓ **Find** the word in each pair of sentences that is missing a capital letter. **Write** that sentence correctly.

5. Are you going to the game with mrs. Frank?
   The game will be on Friday, August 12.

6. I finally met Captain Dale last week.
   He will be here until october 30.

7. Our town has a parade on Veterans day.
   This year it will be on a Wednesday.

8. Was New year's Day always in January?
   No, Mr. Lee said it used to be in March.

Supporting Details

The main idea of a paragraph is what the paragraph is about. The **supporting details** tell more about the main idea. Every sentence in the paragraph should tell a supporting detail.

Read the paragraphs. **Write** the letter of the supporting detail that fits in each paragraph.

> **A** In the winter it was too cold and snowy to play most sports outside.
>
> **B** Often they made patterns of squares, circles, and rings.

1. James Naismith was a gym teacher in Massachusetts. He invented a team sport that his students could play inside.

2. Settlers in the American colonies brought quilting with them from Europe. They sewed scraps of cloth together.

Write a paragraph about a game, sport, or activity. **Use** only details that support your main idea.

Write Facts

> **Writing Prompt** Write facts about a game or sport that you like. You may need to look up facts in books or on the Internet.

All details support the main idea of winning the World Series.

Writer uses capital letters correctly.

An exclamation helps make the paragraph interesting.

Baseball Dream

All baseball fans have one dream. They want their team to win the World Series in October. In the World Series, the best teams from the National League and the American League play each other. The winner is the champion. In 2004 the Boston Red Sox won the World Series. Their fans had been dreaming about this for 86 years! The Red Sox had not won the World Series since 1918.

Quotation Marks

Quotation marks (" ") show the beginning and ending of the words someone says. The speaker's name and words such as **said** or **asked** are not inside the quotation marks.

Kim asked, "What is a symbol?"

"A symbol is something that stands for something else," Jerome said.

A **Write** the sentences. **Add** quotation marks where they are needed.

1. What is a symbol of our country? asked Emma.

2. David said, Our flag is a symbol.

3. The bald eagle is a symbol too, said Liam.

4. Miki asked, Why is the bald eagle a symbol?

5. Sasha said, The bald eagle is strong and free, and so is the United States.

6. Let's find out more about the bald eagle, Alan said.

B **Write** the sentences that use quotation marks correctly.

1. "Plan a Fourth of July party, said Laura."
"Plan a Fourth of July party," said Laura.

2. I have some flags," Ted said.
"I have some flags," Ted said.

3. Jim asked, "Do we have plates with stars?"
"Jim asked, Do we have plates with stars?"

4. Get red, white, and blue balloons, "Vi said."
"Get red, white, and blue balloons," Vi said.

5. "Who is on our list to invite?" asked Ben.
"Who is on our list to invite? asked Ben."

C **Write** each sentence. **Add** quotation marks and a name.

6. Where do we see flags? asked ___.

7. A flag flies outside our school, said ___.

8. I see a flag in our classroom! ___ shouted.

9. ___ stated, The town hall has a flag in front.

10. Do cars ever have flags? ___ asked.

Test Preparation

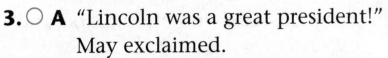

✔ **Mark** the letter of the sentence with the correct quotation marks.

1. ○ **A** "Who were some presidents? asked Ellie."
   ○ **B** "Who were some presidents?" asked Ellie.
   ○ **C** Who were some presidents?" asked Ellie.

2. ○ **A** "Al said, Washington was the first president."
   ○ **B** "Al said," Washington was the first president.
   ○ **C** Al said, "Washington was the first president."

3. ○ **A** "Lincoln was a great president!" May exclaimed.
   ○ **B** "Lincoln was a great president! May exclaimed.
   ○ **C** "Lincoln was a great president! May exclaimed."

4. ○ **A** Was John Adams a president? "asked Abigail."
   ○ **B** "Was John Adams a president?" asked Abigail.
   ○ **C** "Was John Adams a president? asked Abigail."

5. ○ **A** "When was Jimmy Carter president?" asked Bill.
   ○ **B** When was Jimmy Carter president? "asked Bill."
   ○ **C** "When was Jimmy Carter president? asked Bill.

Review

✓ **Write** the sentences. **Add** quotation marks if they are needed. **Write** C after the sentences that are correct.

1. "Who can describe our flag? asked Ms. Lee.

2. Betsy answered, "Well, there are thirteen stripes."

3. Jerry said, The stripes are red and white.

4. "There are fifty white stars in a blue box," Art added.

5. "The stars are in rows, Ross stated."

✓ **Write** the sentences. **Add** quotation marks.

6. Fred asked, Did you know each state has a flag?

7. California's flag has a bear on it, said Mei Ling.

8. Does Arizona's flag have a sunset? Carol asked.

9. Jen stated, Vermont's flag has a pine tree and a cow.

10. Does the Texas flag have a lone star? Sam asked.

Eliminate Wordiness

Don't use more words than are needed.

- Don't use phrases such as *kind of, I think that,* and *it seems like.*
- Don't use *a lot of.* Use *many* or another word.
- Don't use two words that mean the same thing: ~~great~~ *big, tiny* ~~little~~.
- Don't use several words when you can use one word: *moved* ~~with great slowness~~, *moved slowly.*

Rewrite each sentence. **Leave out** or **change** words to eliminate wordiness.

1. The soldiers marched with a great big flag.

2. It seems like the parade took a long time.

3. That flag has a lot of stars on it.

4. The people cheered with great loudness.

5. Lila was kind of excited about the parade.

Write a paragraph about a parade you have seen. **Check** to see that you don't use more words than are needed.

Answer a Question

Writing Prompt   Answer this question: What is something that is important to you? Choose an object or event. Explain why this thing is important.

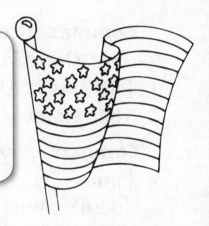

Important thing is named in the opening sentence.

Choice is supported by reasons.

Writer doesn't use more words than are needed.

Our Flag

One thing that is important to me is the flag of the United States. Every time I see it, I think about our country. The flag reminds me that Americans are free. I think about all the people who fought and died to protect that freedom. The flag stands for our country. When people around the world see it, they think about our country too.

Using Commas

Commas are used in addresses:
1501 Greenwood Ave.
Little Rock, AR 72204
Their home is in Niles, Michigan.

Commas are used in dates:
January 31, 1929
Tuesday, June 14

Commas are used to begin and end a letter:
Dear Anna,
Love,
 Krysta

Commas are used to separate three or more things in a sentence:
Krysta wrote letters to Anna, Paul, and Beth.

A **Write** the sentences. **Add** commas where needed. The number in ( ) tells how many commas are needed.

1. Grandma lives in Tampa Florida. (1)

2. Her birthday party was on June 6 2008. (1)

3. She got a hat flowers and cards. (2)

4. We started for home on Sunday June 7. (1)

B **Write** the letter. **Add** commas where needed.

1. 124 Maple Street
Syracuse NY 13210

2. June 24 2009

3. Dear Jaime

4. I am at my grandparents'
ranch in Colorado. We come
here every June. We swim
fish and hike. I see my cousins
aunts and uncles. It is great.
See you soon.

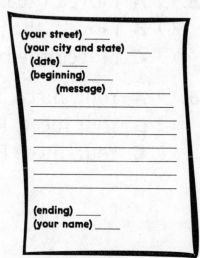

5. Your friend

Tim

C **Write** a letter to a friend about some things you
did together. **Add** commas where needed. **Do not
write** the words in ( ).

6. (your street) ___

(your city and state) ___

7. (date) ___ 2 ___

8. (beginning) Dear ___

9. (message) ___

10. (ending)

(your street) ___
(your city and state) ___
(date) ___
(beginning) ___
(message) _____
_____
_____
_____
_____
_____
(ending) ___
(your name) ___

Test Preparation

☑ **Mark** the letter of the correct answer.

1. ○ **A** Atlanta GA, 30311
   ○ **B** Atlanta, GA, 30311
   ○ **C** Atlanta, GA 30311

2. ○ **A** August 31 2008,
   ○ **B** August 31, 2008
   ○ **C** August, 31 2008

3. ○ **A** Dear Aunt Min,
   ○ **B** Dear, Aunt Min
   ○ **C** Dear Aunt, Min

4. ○ **A** Thanks for the party, gifts and food.
   ○ **B** Thanks for the party, gifts, and, food.
   ○ **C** Thanks for the party, gifts, and food.

5. ○ **A** I loved the peaches, pie, and chicken.
   ○ **B** I loved, the peaches, pie and chicken.
   ○ **C** I loved the peaches, pie, and, chicken.

6. ○ **A** Your, niece, Paula
   ○ **B** Your niece, Paula
   ○ **C** Your, niece Paula

Review

☑ **Write** the sentences. **Add** commas where needed.

1. Tía will visit on Tuesday March 12.

2. She lives in Bisbee Arizona.

3. I will help Mamá clean, shop, and cook.

4. Tía will stay until Friday March 15.

5. Tía wants to ski skate and sled.

☑ **Write** the letter. **Add** commas where needed.

6. 558 Oak Lane
Salina KS 67401

7. October 28 2008

8. Dear Luke

9. Today we had a surprise
party for Mom. I gave her a
card some beads and a rose.
We ate sang and danced.

10. Your friend
Angie

Good Conclusions

> A **good conclusion** wraps up the ideas in a paragraph. It also tries to leave readers with something to think about.

 Write the letter of the stronger conclusion for each paragraph.

1. Our teacher, Ms. Lang, said we could decorate the gym for a costume party. We hung streamers and balloons and gold stars.
   A When people walked in, they cheered and clapped.
   B Everybody liked it.

2. Some people take the same vacation every year. They stay in a cabin by a lake. Often it's the same cabin and the same lake.
   A These people like to be in a familiar place.
   B That sounds boring to me.

 Write a paragraph about a birthday celebration. **Write** a good conclusion.

Write a Report

Writing Prompt Think of an event that happens every year at your school. Write a report about the event. Tell what happens and why.

First sentence tells what the event is. ———

First paragraph describes exactly what a food drive is and why it happens. ———

Writer uses the conclusion to tell why food drives are important. ———

A School Tradition

Every October and May we have a food drive at Bell School. The students bring cans and boxes of food to school. They put the food into bags. A food bank comes to pick up the bags. The workers give the bags to people who need food.

A food drive helps people who do not have enough to eat. It also reminds us how lucky we are.

Commas in Compound Sentences

Sometimes two sentences have ideas that go together. These sentences can be combined using a comma and a connecting word such as **and** or **but.** The combined sentence is called a **compound sentence.**

A cowboy drives the cows to market. His pony helps him.

A cowboy drives the cows to market**, and** his pony helps him.

Cow ponies are small. They are fearless.

Cow ponies are small**, but** they are fearless.

A **Write** each sentence. **Add** a comma where needed. **Circle** the connecting word.

1. Some cowboys rode beside the cows and others rode behind them.

2. There were no roads but there were trails.

3. Cows would get lost and the cowboys would look for them.

4. Longhorns could swim but some of the cowboys couldn't.

B **Use** the word in ( ) and a comma to combine each pair of sentences. **Write** the new sentence.

1. Every summer we get together. Grandpa tells us stories. (and)

2. The night is cool. We get warm by the campfire. (but)

3. We huddle together. We don't say a word. (and)

4. Cindy likes the scary stories. I like the funny ones better. (but)

5. Grandpa uses different voices. He acts out all the parts. (and)

6. He often tells the same stories. We like hearing them again. (but)

C **Complete** the sentences with your ideas. **Add** commas where needed. **Write** the sentences.

7. Rick wants to be a cowboy but I ___.

8. Cowboys eat beans but I eat ___.

9. A cowboy likes a hot bath and I ___.

10. Cowboys work outdoors and I ___.

Test Preparation

✓ **Mark** the letter of the correctly written sentence.

1. ○ **A** A chuckwagon was important and, every trail drive had one.
   ○ **B** A chuckwagon was important, and, every trail drive had one.
   ○ **C** A chuckwagon was important, and every trail drive had one.

2. ○ **A** "Cookie" drove the wagon, and he also made the meals.
   ○ **B** "Cookie" drove the wagon and, he also made the meals.
   ○ **C** "Cookie" drove the wagon, and, he also made the meals.

3. ○ **A** Food was in sacks and drawers but, water was in a barrel.
   ○ **B** Food was in sacks and drawers, but water was in a barrel.
   ○ **C** Food was in sacks and drawers, water was in a barrel.

4. ○ **A** The beans were tasty, and the biscuits were hot.
   ○ **B** The beans were tasty, the biscuits were hot.
   ○ **C** The beans were tasty, but, the biscuits were hot.

Review

✓ **Write** the sentences. **Underline** the connecting words. **Add** commas where needed.

1. Cowboys get up early and they work hard all day.

2. Some ranchers raise cattle but others raise sheep.

3. Cowboys wear bandanas but businessmen wear ties.

4. Cattle have sharp horns and deer have sharp antlers.

5. A cowboy uses a rope but a carpenter uses a hammer.

✓ **Use** the word in ( ) and a comma to combine each pair of sentences. **Write** the new sentence.

6. Penny has boots. She needs a hat. (but)

7. Jason's belt is brown leather. It has a shiny buckle. (and)

8. Alex loves her baseball shirt. It is torn. (but)

9. Kiki lost her vest. Her dad found it. (but)

10. Jay bought a bandana. He wore it today. (and)

Topic Sentences

A **topic sentence** tells the main idea of a paragraph. The topic sentence is often the first sentence of the paragraph.

 Write the letter of the topic sentence that should begin each paragraph.

> **A** Chefs are cooks and leaders.
> **B** Cowhands today are like cowhands long ago.

1. ___ They work on ranches and take care of cattle. They rope cows and ride horses. They work in all kinds of weather.

2. ___ At fancy restaurants, they plan menus and cook food. They also check the work of the other cooks.

 Write a paragraph about a job that someone you know has. **Begin** with a topic sentence that tells the main idea of the paragraph.

Write a Job Description

Writing Prompt Write a description of a job. Tell what the job is and what kind of person would be good at this job.

Main idea is stated in topic sentence at beginning of paragraph.

All other sentences give details that support the main idea.

Strong conclusion leaves readers with something to think about.

A Pilot's Job

Pilots have a very important job. They fly airplanes filled with people. The people depend on pilots to get them safely from one place to another. Pilots need to be calm, smart, and brave. They must take care of any problems, and they can't make any mistakes. A mistake could hurt people.

The Paragraph

A **paragraph** is a group of sentences about the same idea. The sentences are in an order that makes sense. One sentence gives the main idea. The other sentences give details about the main idea. The first sentence of a paragraph is indented.

Carmen has a piñata at her birthday party. It is shaped like a horse. It has paper streamers for its mane and tail. The piñata is beautiful.

A **Write** the sentences. **Write** *1*, *2*, *3*, *4*, or *5* after each sentence to show the correct order for a paragraph.

1. The piñata breaks, and treats fall out.

2. She misses the piñata the first time.

3. This time she hits the piñata!

4. Carmen swings a stick at the piñata.

5. Carmen swings the stick again.

B **Write** the sentences in the correct order to make a paragraph. **Indent** the first sentence. **Underline** the main idea sentence.

1. Grandma showed me how to dance.

2. The next week I practiced for many hours.

3. At last I was ready for the talent show.

4. Then I tried the dance as she watched.

5. First I watched her do the dance steps.

C **Decide** which sentence does not belong. **Write** the other sentences in the correct order to make a paragraph. **Indent** the first sentence.

6. Afterwards, we always have a meal with our friends.

7. Our whole family likes going to the talent show.

8. I have two dance costumes.

9. First we look around for seats.

10. Then we sit and watch the show.

Test Preparation

✓ **Read** the paragraph. **Mark** the letter of the correct answer to each question.

Sun and Moon race in the sky every day. Sun climbs high and later dips out of sight. Sun peeks out early in the morning. When it is dark, Moon comes after Sun. Then it starts to rain. But Moon never catches up.

1. What was done to the first sentence?

○ **A** It was kept long.
○ **B** It had quotation marks added.
○ **C** It was indented.

2. Which sentence gives the main idea?

○ **A** Sun and Moon race in the sky every day.
○ **B** But Moon never catches up.
○ **C** Then it starts to rain.

3. Which sentence does not belong?

○ **A** When it is dark, Moon comes after Sun.
○ **B** Then it starts to rain.
○ **C** Sun climbs high and later dips out of sight.

4. Which sentence is out of order?

○ **A** Sun peeks out early in the morning.
○ **B** When it is dark, Moon comes after Sun.
○ **C** But Moon never catches up.

Review

☑ **Write** the sentences in the correct order to make a paragraph. **Indent** the first sentence. **Underline** the main idea sentence.

1. We celebrate Thanksgiving with relatives.

2. Their son, my cousin Al, comes with them.

3. When the last person gets there, we eat.

4. First my aunt and uncle arrive.

5. Soon afterwards, Grandpa drives over.

☑ **Decide** which sentence does not belong. **Write** the other sentences in the correct order to make a paragraph. **Indent** the first sentence.

6. Grandpa makes wonderful things.

7. Next week he plans to make a drum.

8. Tomorrow he will build a wagon.

9. Grandma is a good painter.

10. Right now he is making a wooden yo-yo.

Good Paragraphs

- In a good **paragraph**, all the sentences tell about the same idea.
- One sentence gives the main idea, and the other sentences give details about it.
- The sentences are in an order that makes sense.
- The first sentence is indented.

 Read the sentences below. **Decide** which sentence does not tell about the same idea. **Write** the other sentences in the correct order to make a paragraph. **Indent** the first sentence.

She cuts out large red paper hearts.

Every year Mom and I make valentines.

I get many valentines from my friends.

We write messages on the hearts.

Then we give our valentines to our friends.

 Write a paragraph about something your family does on a holiday or other special occasion.

Describe a Tradition

Writing Prompt Write about the things you do to celebrate Thanksgiving at school and at home.

All sentences in each paragraph tell about the same idea.

First sentence in each paragraph is indented.

Writer uses the conclusion to summarize ideas.

Thanksgiving

At school we learn about the first Thanksgiving. The Pilgrims wanted to celebrate a good harvest. They invited the Indians to dinner.

On Thanksgiving Day we celebrate too. We eat turkey, sweet potatoes, cranberry sauce, green beans, and pumpkin pie. Many relatives come to our house. I get to play with my four cousins. We play football or watch it on television.

History, food, family, and football are all part of our Thanksgiving.

Taking Tests

Follow these tips when writing for a test:

Before Writing

• Read the prompt carefully. Think about what it asks you to do.
• Write down key words. For example, here is a prompt:
    Write a <u>thank you letter</u> to a <u>friend</u>.
The key words tell you to write a letter to thank a friend. You will use the letter form and thank someone in a friendly voice.
• Use a graphic organizer to plan your composition.

During Writing

• Keep the prompt in mind to stay on the topic.
• Follow your graphic organizer. Stay focused.
• Write a good beginning. You might ask readers a question or give an interesting fact.
• Support your main idea.
• Write a strong ending. You might add a final comment of your own or give your reader a command.

After Writing

• Check grammar, punctuation, and spelling.
• Are there places that need more details or clearer information?

Writing a Story About Me

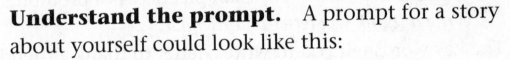

A **test** may ask you to write a story about yourself. It should have a beginning, middle, and end.

Understand the prompt. A prompt for a story about yourself could look like this:

> Write about a time you were surprised. Tell how you felt. Your story should have a beginning, middle, and end.

Key phrases are *you were surprised, how you felt*, and *beginning, middle, and end.*

Find a good topic. Choose something that you remember well. Make sure you can tell about the beginning, middle, and end of the story.

Organize your ideas. Make a list of details. Then put them in order. Tell how you felt.

My Birthday Surprise	
Nobody talked to me.	Felt sad
Doorbell rang	Friends came over.

Write a good beginning. Tell the reader what you're writing about in your first sentence.

Develop and elaborate ideas. Use the details in your list. Use words that show your feelings.

Write a strong ending. Tell how the event ends.

Check your work. Make changes if you need to.

See how the personal story below follows the prompt.

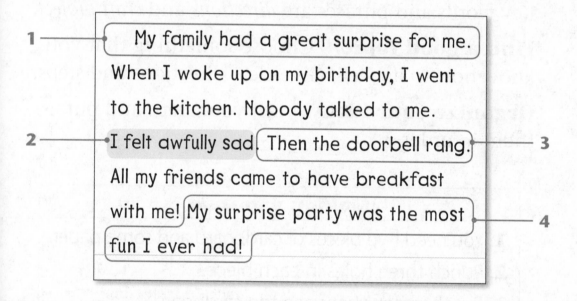

1 — My family had a great surprise for me. When I woke up on my birthday, I went to the kitchen. Nobody talked to me.

2 — I felt awfully sad. Then the doorbell rang. — 3

All my friends came to have breakfast with me! My surprise party was the most — 4

fun I ever had!

1. The first sentence organizes the entire piece.

2. The writer tells how he or she felt.

3. Events are in order; clue word *then* is used.

4. The ending sentence wraps up the story.

Writing a How-To Report

A **test** may ask you to write a how-to report. Include all the steps. Use order words such as *first* and *then*.

Understand the prompt. Read the prompt again. Here is a prompt for a how-to report:

Write directions for a craft project you do in school.

Key words and phrases are *directions* and *craft project*.

Find a good topic. Choose something that you know how to do well. Give clear directions and steps.

Organize your ideas. List your steps and put them in order.

Making a Journal
1. You need two pieces of cardboard and some paper.
2. Punch three holes in each piece.
3. Put the paper between the cardboard.
4. Tie the pieces together and decorate the cover.

Write a good beginning. Explain what you are writing about in your first sentence.

Develop and elaborate ideas. Add details so readers know exactly what to do.

Write a strong ending. Tell what you think.

Check your work. Make any changes.

See how the how-to report below follows the prompt.

Did you know that you can make your own journal? You will need two pieces of cardboard and some sheets of blank paper. First, carefully punch three holes in each piece of cardboard and paper. Then slide the paper between the cardboard pieces. Last, tie all the pieces together and decorate the cover. This is a great place to write all your ideas.

1. Product and materials are given first.

2. Order words tell when to do each step.

3. Adjectives and adverbs give information.

4. The ending wraps up the ideas in the report.

Writing a Compare/Contrast Paragraph

A **test** may ask you to write a compare/contrast paragraph. Tell how things are the same and different.

Understand the prompt. A prompt that asks you to write a compare/contrast paragraph could look like this:

Write about something you did in the past that you still do now. Tell how what you did has changed and how it has stayed the same.

Key phrases are *did in the past* and *do now*.

Find a good topic. Think of things you do.

Organize your ideas. Make a diagram.

Write a good beginning. A good opening sentence will make your reader want to read more.

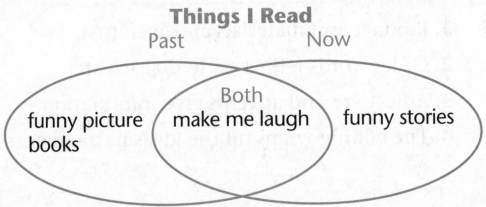

Things I Read

Past   Now

Both

funny picture books   make me laugh   funny stories

Develop and elaborate ideas. Use the details from your diagram to talk about then and now.

Write a strong ending. Sum up your ideas.

Check your work. Make changes as needed.

See how the paragraph below tells how the topic is the same and different.

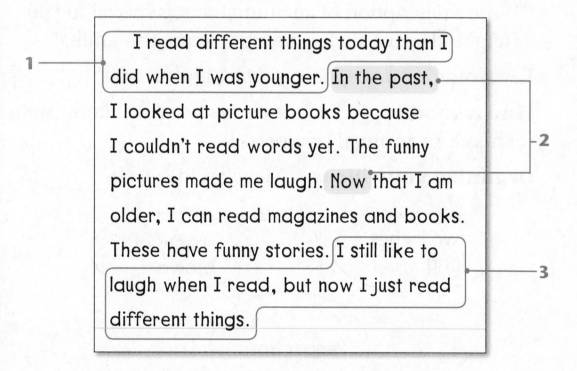

1.
I read different things today than I did when I was younger. In the past, I looked at picture books because I couldn't read words yet. The funny pictures made me laugh. Now that I am older, I can read magazines and books. These have funny stories. I still like to laugh when I read, but now I just read different things.

2.

3.

1. The first sentence states the main idea.

2. The writer tells when something happened.

3. The ending tells what is alike and different.

Writing a Descriptive Paragraph

A **test** may ask you to write a description. Use exciting words that make readers use their senses.

Understand the prompt. A prompt for a description could look like this:

> Write a description of an animal that is special to you. Help readers use their senses to picture this animal.

Key words are *description, animal,* and *senses*.

Find a good topic. Choose an animal you know well, such as a zoo animal or a pet.

Organize your ideas. Make an idea web.

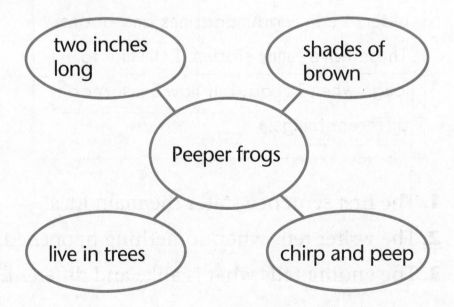

two inches long

shades of brown

Peeper frogs

live in trees

chirp and peep

Write a good beginning. Set up your topic.

Develop ideas. Paint word pictures.

Write a strong ending. Address your readers.

Check your work. Have you used the best words?

See how the description below answers the prompt.

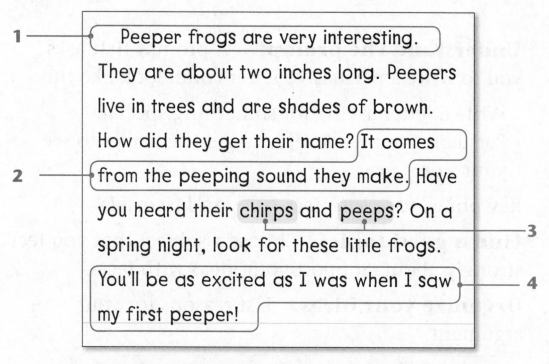

1. — Peeper frogs are very interesting. They are about two inches long. Peepers live in trees and are shades of brown. How did they get their name? It comes — 2. from the peeping sound they make. Have you heard their chirps and peeps? On a — 3 spring night, look for these little frogs. You'll be as excited as I was when I saw — 4 my first peeper!

1. The first sentence states the topic clearly.

2. This is an important detail.

3. Specific nouns add to the word picture.

4. The strong ending shows the writer's feelings.

Writing a Persuasive Letter

A **test** may ask you to write a persuasive letter. Support your ideas with examples, facts, and reasons. Use words such as *should* and *most important*. Follow the tips below.

Understand the prompt. A prompt that asks you to write a persuasive letter could look like this:

> Write a letter asking for something special. Persuade your reader. Try to get the reader to see your side.

Key phrases are *letter, persuade,* and *your side.*

Find a good topic. Choose a subject that you feel strongly about. Support your ideas with facts.

Organize your ideas. List reasons for your argument.

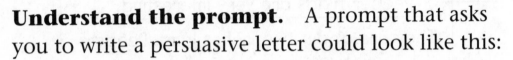

Getting a New Bike
My old bike is too small.
I worked and saved money.
I have enough money to buy a new bike.
A new bike will be safer.

Write a good beginning. Tell the reader what you want in the first sentence.

Develop and elaborate ideas. Use facts to support your argument. Use words such as *should* or *best*.

Write a strong ending. Sum up your reasons.

Check your work. Make any necessary changes.

See how the persuasive letter below follows the prompt.

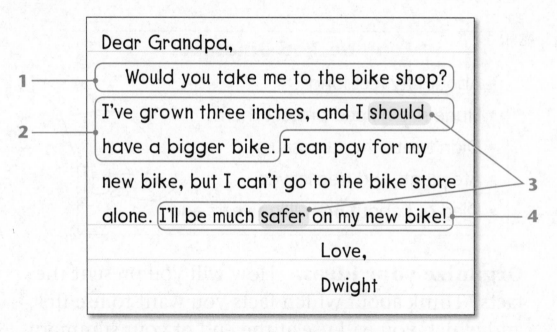

Dear Grandpa,

1 — Would you take me to the bike shop?

2 — I've grown three inches, and I should have a bigger bike. I can pay for my new bike, but I can't go to the bike store alone. I'll be much safer on my new bike! — 3, 4

Love,

Dwight

1. First sentence states argument.

2. Facts and reasons support argument.

3. Words such as *should* and *safer* are persuasive.

4. Ending sentence gives strongest reason.

Writing a Summary

Some **tests** may ask you to write a summary from a list of facts, a time line, or a chart. You will need to read the information carefully and use it in your own sentences. Follow the tips below.

Long-Necked Dinosaurs
• About fifty feet long
• Huge size helped protect them
• Didn't eat other dinosaurs
• Ate plants and tree leaves
• Died out about 64 million years ago

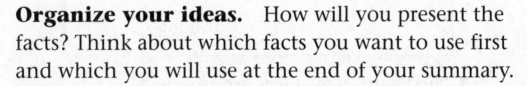

Organize your ideas.   How will you present the facts? Think about which facts you want to use first and which you will use at the end of your summary.

Write a good beginning.   Write an interesting beginning sentence that makes your readers want to keep reading. Think of a topic sentence that presents the main idea clearly.

Develop and elaborate ideas. Make sure the details support your main idea.

Write a strong ending. Write sentences that pull the information together.

Check your work. Make any necessary changes.

See how the report below summarizes information.

1 — Which dinosaur is your favorite? Mine is the long-necked dinosaur. Head to

2 — tail it was about fifty feet long. That's — 3
almost as tall as a five-story building!

This dinosaur's huge size helped protect it from enemies. These plant eaters died about sixty-four million years ago. I think

it is sad that now we can see these giant — 4
animals only in pictures and museums.

1. The first sentence grabs the reader's attention.

2. The writer paints a picture for the reader.

3. Pronouns and contractions are correct.

4. The last sentence shows the writer's feelings.

Grammar Patrol

Grammar Patrol

adjective   An **adjective** describes a person, place, animal, or thing. An adjective can tell how something looks, sounds, tastes, feels, or smells.

> I love **warm** cookies.
> (**Warm** describes the way the cookies feel.)

- Words for number, size, and shape are adjectives. The words **a** and **an** are also adjectives. Use **a** before a word that begins with a consonant sound. Use **an** before a word with a vowel sound.

> My sister wrote **a** letter.
> Dad gave her **an** envelope.

> (The word **a** describes how many letters—one.
> The word **an** describes how many envelopes–one.)

> My sister wrote a **long** letter.
> (**Long** describes the size of the letter.)

- Add **–er** to an adjective to **compare** two persons, places, or things.

> Mark is tall**er** than I am.

- Add **–est** to an adjective to **compare** three or more persons, places, or things.

> Sarah is the tall**est** girl in the class.

adverb   An **adverb** tells more about a verb.

- Some adverbs tell **when**.

  We're going to the museum **tomorrow**.

- Some adverbs tell **where**.

  We waited **inside**.

- Some adverbs tell **how.** Many adverbs that tell **how** end in **–ly**.

  I ate the ice cream **quickly.**

contraction   A contraction is a short way to put two words together. An apostrophe **(')** takes the place of one or more letters.

- Contractions can be formed by putting together a pronoun and another word, such as **will, are,** or **is.**

  I will see the movie tomorrow.
  I'll see the movie tomorrow.

- Many contractions are formed with verbs and the word **not.**

  I **did not** bring my music.
  I **didn't** bring my music.

noun   A **noun** names a person, place, animal, or thing.

  My **brother** takes **lunch** to **school.**
  (person)   (thing)   (place)

- To make most nouns **plural**, add **-s.**

  pencil + s = pencils   horse + s = horses

- Some nouns add **–es** to form the **plural.** These nouns end in **ss, x, ch,** or **sh.**

  class + es = classes   lunch + es = lunches
  fox + es = foxes   bush + es = bushes

- Some nouns change their spelling to form the **plural.**

Singular	Plural
child	children
man	men
woman	women
foot	feet
tooth	teeth
goose	geese
mouse	mice

- **Proper nouns** are special names for people, places, animals, and things. They begin with capital letters. **Days of the week, months of the year,** and **holidays** also begin with capital letters. Titles for people begin with capital letters. Many titles end with a period **(.)**.

  Heather Frank plays in the band.
  Ms. Young is the director.
  The first concert is at **Jones School** on **Sunday, March** 20.

- **Possessive nouns** show ownership. Many nouns add an **apostrophe** and **s ('s)** to show ownership.

  The trunk of the elephant is very long.
  The elephant**'s** trunk is very long.

- Many **plural possessive nouns** add only an **apostrophe (')** to show ownership.

  The girls**'** shoes are new.

pronoun   A **pronoun** takes the place of a noun.

- **He, she,** and **it** are pronouns that name only one. **We** and **they** are pronouns that name more than one.

    David likes games.
    He likes board games.

    David and Chris play chess.
    They play chess.

- The pronouns **I** and **me** take the place of your name. Use **I** in the subject of a sentence. Use **me** after an action verb. Always write **I** with a capital letter.

    I walk to school. Scott walks with **me.**

When you talk about yourself and another person, name yourself last. The pronouns **I** and **me** take the place of your name.

    Jane and **I** play after school.
    My mom drives Jane and **me** home.

The pronouns **I, he, she, we** and **they** are used as subjects of sentences. The pronouns **me, him, her, us,** and **them** are used after action verbs. The pronouns **you** and **it** can be used anywhere in a sentence.

Ned bakes a cake. **He** frosts **it.**
Paul sees Jill. He waves to **her.**

- The pronoun **me** is used in the telling part of a sentence.

They waited for **me.**

sentence   A sentence tells a complete idea. It begins with a capital letter.

My grandmother makes good cookies.

- A **telling sentence**, or **statement**, ends with a **period (.)**.

Tim played the violin quietly**.**

- An **asking sentence**, or **question**, ends with a **question mark (?)**.

Are you coming over**?**

- A **command** gives an order. It ends with a period **(.)**.

Wash your hands**.**

- An **exclamation** shows strong feeling. It ends with an exclamation mark **(!)**.

   What a beautiful day it is**!**

- A sentence has two parts. It has a **subject** and a **predicate.**

   The girl sings a song.

   The girl   names who the sentence is about (subject)

   sings a song.   tells what the girl does (predicate)

- The words in a sentence must be in an order that makes sense.

   By ate We campfire. The hot dogs   is not a sentence

   We ate hot dogs by the campfire.   is a sentence

- The meaning of a sentence changes if the word order changes.

   The **bag** is in the **box**.
   The **box** is in the **bag**.
   Is the **box** in the **bag**?

- A **compound sentence** has two simple sentences joined by the word **and, but,** or **or**. Use a comma in a compound sentence before the word **and, but,** or **or**.

verb   A word that tells what someone or something does is a verb.

JoAnn **reads.**   Jeff **rides** his bike.

- A verb can tell what one person, animal, or thing does. Add **–s** to show what is being done now.

The rabbit **hops.**

- Do not add **–s** to a verb that tells what two or more people, animals, or things do now.

Tim and Tom **clean** their room.

- Verbs can tell what happens **now,** what happened in the **past,** or what will happen in the **future.**

Today Margie **bakes** bread.
(The verb **bakes** tells about now. It ends with **–s.**)

Yesterday Margie **baked** bread.
(The verb **baked** tells about the past. It ends with **–ed.**)

Tomorrow Margie **will bake** bread.
(The verb **will bake** tells about the future. It begins with **will.**)

- The verbs **am, is, are, was,** and **were** do not show action. They show what someone or something is or was.

The baby **is tired.** Greg **was angry.**

The verbs **am, is,** and **are** tell about now.

I **am** a nurse. Jose **is** a nurse. Jo and Dan **are** nurses.

The verbs **was** and **were** tell about the past.

I **was** thirsty. He **was** thirsty. We **were** thirsty.

Use **am, is,** and **was** to tell about one person, place, or thing. Use **are** and **were** to tell about more than one person, place, or thing.

Capitalization

sentence   A sentence begins with a capital letter.

The woman is tall.

names for people, places, and pets   The names of people, places, and pets begin with capital letters.

Beth Cane and her bird Milly live in Denver.

titles for people   Titles for people begin with capital letters. Most titles end with a period.

Mr. Lee ate dinner with Dr. Sanchez and Ms. Fields.

days of the week   The names of the days of the week begin with capital letters.

Our game is on Saturday.

months and holidays   The names of months and holidays begin with capital letters.

I know that Martin Luther King, Jr., Day is in January.

using I   The pronoun I is always used in the subject of a sentence. Always write I with a capital letter. Always name yourself last.

Liz and I looked for shells.

Punctuation

period   Use a period **(.)** at the end of a sentence.

Robbie plays catch with his dad**.**

- Use a period at the end of a command.

Stay on the sidewalk**.**

- Most titles for people end with a period.

Mr**.** Lee ate lunch with Dr**.** King and Ms**.** Bell.

question mark   Use a question mark **(?)** at the end of a question.

Where is your brother**?**

exclamation mark   Use an exclamation mark **(!)** at the end of an exclamation.

What a day we had**!**

quotation marks   Quotation marks show the beginning and ending of the words someone says. The speaker's name and words such as **said** or **asked** are not inside the quotation marks.

"Let's go to the zoo," said Marla.
Brian asked, "What is your favorite animal?"

apostrophe   Use an apostrophe **(')** to take the place of one or more letters in a contraction. A contraction is a short way to put two words together.

is + not = isn't   **we + will = we'll**

- Use an apostrophe (**'**) and **s** to show ownership.

  The trunk of an elephant can hold water.
  The elephant**'s** trunk can hold water.

commas

- Commas (**,**) are used in addresses:

  Durham, NC

- Commas are used in dates:

  August 23, 1957   Saturday, April 12

- Commas are used to begin and end a letter:

  Dear Aunt May,
  Love,
      Josh

- Commas are used to separate three things in a sentence.

  Kate ate cereal, toast, and a banana.

- Use a comma before the word **and** or **but** in a compound sentence.

  Liam plays the trumpet, **and** he plays soccer.
  Jack goes to the movies, **but** Lisa stays home.

Frequently Misspelled Words

For many writers, some words are difficult to spell. You can use this list to check your spelling.

a lot	eat	into	party	thought
about	end	is	people	through
again	every	it's	play	to
all	everybody	knew	presents	too
always	family	know	pretty	took
and	favorite	like	put	tried
another	find	little	really	two
are	first	live	said	under
as	for	look	saw	upon
away	found	love	scared	use
baseball	friend	make	school	very
be	from	many	see	want
beautiful	get	more	so	was
because	girl	my	some	watch
before	give	new	sometimes	we
birthday	go	nice	special	went
brother	going	night	started	were
but	good	not	swimming	what
by	Halloween	now	thank	when
came	has	of	that	where
caught	have	on	that's	who
Christmas	heard	once	the	whole
come	her	one	their	will
could	here	or	them	with
didn't	him	other	then	would
different	his	our	there	you
do	home	out	there's	your
does	house	outside	these	
don't	how	over	they	
down	I	part	they're	

D'Nealian™ Alphabet

a b c d e f g h i
j k l m n o p q r s t
u v w x y z

A B C D E F G
H I J K L M N O
P Q R S T U V
W X Y Z . , ' ?

1 2 3 4 5 6
7 8 9 10

Manuscript Alphabet

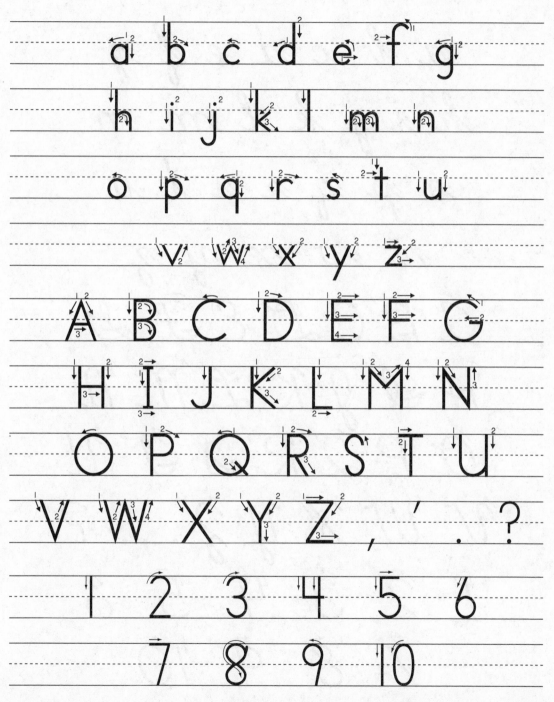

Cursive Alphabet

a b c d e f g

h i j k l m n

o p q r s t u

v w x y z

A B C D E F G

H I J K L M N

O P Q R S T U

V W X Y Z . , ' ?

1 2 3 4 5 6

7 8 9 10

Index

A

Action verbs. *See* Verbs.

Addresses. *See* Commas.

Adjectives, 140–143, 245

    a and *an,* 146–149

    and our senses, 140–143

    for number, size, and shape, 146–149

    that compare, 152–155

Adverbs, 158–161, 246

    that tell how, 164–167

    that tell when and where, 158–161

Agreement, subject-verb, 116–119

Am, is, are, was, were, 134–137

Apostrophe

    in contractions, 194–197

    in possessive nouns, 104–107

B

Be, 134–137

C

Capital letters, 254

    days of week, 86–89, 200–203

first word of sentence, 50–53, 68–71

holidays, 86–89

months of year, 86–89, 200–203

proper nouns, 86–89

titles for people, 86–89, 200–203

Check own writing, 46–48

Combining sentences, 218–221

Commands. *See* Sentences.

Commas

    addresses, 212–215

    dates, 212–215

    in compound sentences, 218–221

    in letters, 212–215

    to separate three or more things, 212–215

Compound sentences. *See* Sentences.

Contractions, 194–197, 246–247

Conventions. *See* Writing.

D

Dates. *See* Commas.

Days of week, 86–89, 200–203

end marks, 50–53, 68–71,
74–77, 78, 126

exclamations, 74–77, 78, 126

predicates, 62–65, 66

questions, 68–71, 126

statements, 68–71, 126

subjects, 56–59, 60

topic, 222

Singular nouns. *See* Nouns. *See also* Verbs.

Statements. *See* Sentences.

Strategies. *See* Writing.

Subjects, 56–59, 60

Subject-verb agreement, 116–119

T

Tenses, 122–125

Test preparation, 52, 58, 64, 70, 76, 82, 88, 94, 100, 106, 112, 118, 124, 130, 136, 142, 148, 154, 160, 166, 172, 178, 184, 190, 196, 202, 208, 214, 220, 226

Tests. *See* Writing for tests.

Time-order words. *See* Writing.

Titles for people, 86–89, 200–203

V

Verbs, 110–113, 252–253

action, 110–113

agreement, 116–119

am, is, are, was, were, 134–137

to be, 134–137

future tense, 122–125, 128–131

past tense, 122–125, 128–131

present tense, 122–125, 128–131

with plural nouns, 116–119

with singular nouns, 116–119

Voice. *See* Writing.

W

Word choice. *See* Writing.

Writer's craft. *See topics under* Writing. *See also main entries.*

Writing

commands and exclamations, 78

conventions, 22–25

descriptive words in predicates, 66

descriptive words in subjects, 60

details, 2–3, 204